T0220207

Developing for Apple TV using tvOS and Swift

Gary Bennett
Stefan Kaczmarek
Brad Lees

Apress®

Developing for Apple TV using tvOS and Swift

ISBN-13 (pbk): 978-1-4842-1714-6

ISBN-13 (electronic): 978-1-4842-1715-3

Managing Director: Welmoed Spahr
Lead Editor: Michelle Lowman
Development Editor: James Markham
Editorial Board: Steve Anglin, Louise Corrigan, James DeWolf, Jonathan Gennick,
    Robert Hutchinson, Michelle Lowman, James Markham, Susan McDermott,
    Matthew Moodie, Jeffrey Pepper, Douglas Pundick, Ben Renow-Clarke, Gwenan Spearing
Coordinating Editors: Mark Powers
Copy Editor: Mary Bearden
Compositor: SPi Global
Indexer: SPi Global
Artist: SPi Global

Distributed to the book trade worldwide by Springer Science+Business Media New York, 233 Spring Street, 6th Floor, New York, NY 10013. Phone 1-800-SPRINGER, fax (201) 348-4505, e-mail orders-ny@springer-sbm.com, or visit www.springeronline.com. Apress Media, LLC is a California LLC and the sole member (owner) is Springer Science + Business Media Finance Inc (SSBM Finance Inc). SSBM Finance Inc is a Delaware corporation.

For information on translations, please e-mail rights@apress.com, or visit www.apress.com.

Apress and friends of ED books may be purchased in bulk for academic, corporate, or promotional use. eBook versions and licenses are also available for most titles. For more information, reference our Special Bulk Sales–eBook Licensing web page at www.apress.com/bulk-sales.

Any source code or other supplementary material referenced by the author in this text is available to readers at www.apress.com/9781484217146 or http://forum.xcelme.com. For detailed information about how to locate your book's source code, go to www.apress.com/source-code/. Readers can also access source code at SpringerLink in the Supplementary Material section for each chapter.

Gary would like to dedicate this book to wife Stefanie and children, Michael, Danielle, Michelle, and Emily, for always supporing him.

Stefan would like to dedicate this book to his wife Veronica for supporting him throughout all of life's adventures.

Brad would like to dedicate this book to his wife Natalie for always supporting him. He couldn't do it without her.

Contents at a Glance

Contents

About the Authors

Gary Bennett is president of xcelMe.com, which provides iOS programming courses online. By day, Gary develops iOS apps professionally, and by night, he teaches iOS programming. For more than six years, Gary has taught thousands of students how to develop iPhone/iPad apps and has several popular apps in the iTunes App Store. Gary has a bachelor's degree in computer science and has worked for 25 years in the technology and defense industries. He served 10 years in the U.S. Navy as a nuclear engineer aboard two nuclear submarines. After leaving the Navy, Gary worked for several companies as a software developer, CIO, and president. As CIO, he helped take VistaCare public in 2002. Gary also coauthored two editions of *Objective-C for Absolute Beginners* and *iPhone Cool Projects* for Apress. He lives in Scottsdale, Arizona, with his wife Stefanie and their four children.

Stefan Kaczmarek has more than 15 years of software development experience specializing in mobile applications, large-scale software systems, project management, network protocols, encryption algorithms, and audio/video codecs. As chief software architect and cofounder of SKJM, LLC, Stefan developed a number of successful mobile applications including iCam (which has been featured on CNN, *Good Morning America*, and *The Today Show*, and which was chosen by Apple to be featured in the "Dog Lover" iPhone 3GS television commercial) and iSpy Cameras (which held the #1 Paid iPhone App ranking in a number of countries around the world including the United Kingdom, Ireland, Italy, Sweden, and South Korea). Stefan resides in Phoenix, Arizona, with his wife, Veronica, and their two children.

Brad Lees has more than 16 years of experience in application development and server management. He has specialized in creating and initiating software programs in financial institutions, credit card processing, point-of-sale systems, and real estate development.

His professional career highlights have been lead iOS developer at Apriva, owner of Innovativeware, product development manager for Smarsh, and vice president of application development for iNation. Brad also coauthored two editions of *Objective-C for Absolute Beginners.*

A graduate of Arizona State University, Brad and his wife Natalie reside in Phoenix with their five children.

Acknowledgments

We would like to thank Apress for all their help in making this book possible. Specifically, we would like to thank Mark Powers, our coordinating editor, and Michelle Lowman, our acquisitions editor, for helping us stay focused and overcoming many obstacles. Without Mark and Michelle, this book would not have been possible.

Special thanks to Jim Markham, our development editor, for all his suggestions during the editorial review process to help make this a great book. Thanks to Mary Bearden, the copy editor, who made the book look great.

We would like to thank the CodeRed-I creative design team for their visual design direction to complete the fresh, stylized front and back cover. Special thanks to Giang Le for his contemporary and retro graphic design elements.

Introduction

We are now able to write apps for the new Apple TV. This is great for iOS developers because everything is very familiar. Xcode, Swift, UIKit Interface Builder and the tvOS Simulator are very similar to iOS development.

This book assumes you are very familiar with iOS development using Swift. If you are not, please read our *Swift 2 for Absolute Beginners* from Apress (`www.apress.com/9781484214893`).

Swift 2 for Absolute Beginners takes you through all the development to get you up to speed to become a tvOS developer and how to do it.

Free Live Webinars, Q&A, and YouTube Videos

Every other Monday night at 6:00 p.m. Pacific time, we have live webinars and discuss a topic from the book or a timely item of interest. These webinars are free, and you can register for them at `www.xcelme.com/latest-videos/`.

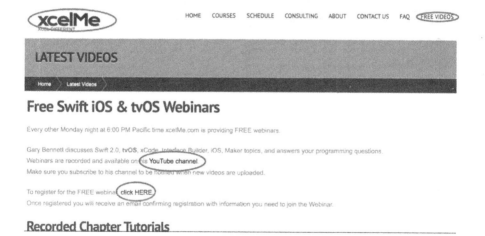

At the end of the webinars, we have a Q&A. You can ask a question on the topic discussed or on any topic in the book.

Additionally, all these webinars are recorded and available on YouTube. Make sure you subscribe to the YouTube channel so you are notified when new recordings are uploaded.

Free Book Forum

We have provided an online forum for this book at http://forum.xcelme.com, where you can ask questions while you are learning Swift and get answers from the authors. Also, Apple makes frequent changes to the programming language and SDK. We try our best to make sure any changes affecting the book are updated on the forum along with any significant text or code changes.

You can download the source code from the chapters on this forum too.

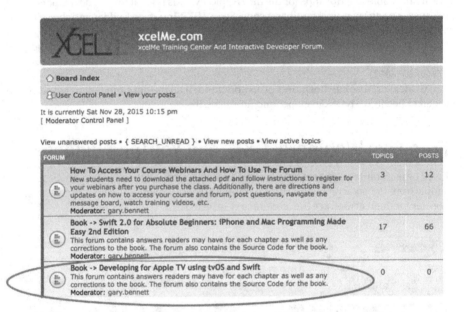

■ ■ ■

CHAPTER 1

Getting Started with the New Apple TV

Finally! For years iOS developers have been waiting to write apps for the Apple TV. Three years ago, we read in Steve Jobs's biography that Apple had been working on a new Apple TV, and the current Apple TV was "just a hobby." In the summer of 2015, Apple finally announced the new Apple TV along with the operating system called tvOS. Developers can now write apps for the Apple TV, and there is a new App Store for tvOS apps.

■ **Note** If you haven't already read the Introduction to this book, take the time to do so. The Introduction covers how to access the free tvOS forum, source code used in this book, free YouTube tvOS training videos, and how to learn Swift 2.

Lots of Good News

There are a lot of great things about the Apple TV. It is important that you understand what the Apple TV is capable of so that you can use these capabilities in your tvOS apps.

Capabilities

The capabilities of the new Apple TV include:

- 64-bit A8 processor
- 32GB or 64GB of storage
- 2GB of RAM
- 10/100 Mbps Ethernet
- Wi-Fi 802.11a/b/g/n/ac
- 1080p resolution

- HDMI
- New Siri Remote/Apple TV Remote
- Bluetooth capability

Inherited iOS Frameworks

Many of the frameworks available for iOS are available for tvOS. These include:

- Accelerate
- AudioToolbox
- AudioUnit
- AVFoundation
- AVKit
- CFNetwork
- CloudKit
- CoreBluetooth
- CoreData
- CoreFoundation
- CoreGraphics
- CoreImage
- CoreLocation
- CoreMedia
- CoreSpotlight
- CoreText
- CoreVideo
- Darwin
- Foundation
- GameController
- GameKit

- GameplayKit
- GLKit
- ImageIO
- MachO
- MediaAccessibility
- MediaPlayer
- MediaToolbox
- Metal
- MetalKit
- MetalPerformanceShaders
- MobileCoreServices
- ModelIO
- OpenGLES
- SceneKit
- Security
- simd
- SpriteKit
- StoreKit
- Swift Standard Library
- SystemConfiguration
- UIKit

The Apple A8 Processor

The Apple TV processor is a 64-bit ARM-based system on a chip (SoC) designed by Apple and manufactured by TSMC. It contains two billion transistors, twice as many as the previous A7 processor.

The A8 processor was first introduced in the iPhone 6 and iPhone 6 Plus. The A8 has 25% more CPU performance and 50% more graphics performance while drawing only 50% of the power compared to its predecessor, the A7 (see Figure 1-1).

Figure 1-1. *Apple's A8 processor, used in the fourth-generation Apple TV*

3

The Siri Remote

The Siri Remote has the following buttons (see Figure 1-2):

1. *Touch surface.* Swipe to navigate. Press to select. Press and hold for contextual menus.

2. *Menu.* Press to return to the previous menu.

3. *Siri/Search.* Press and hold to talk in those countries that have the Siri Remote. In all other countries, press to open the onscreen search app.

4. *Play/Pause.* Play and pause media.

5. *Home.* Press to return to the Home screen. Press twice to view open apps. Press and hold to sleep.

6. *Volume.* Control TV volume.

7. *Lightning connector.* Plug-in for charging

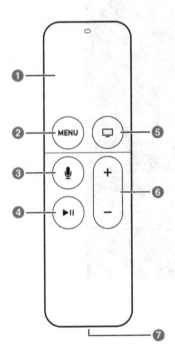

Figure 1-2. Apple's Siri Remote

Apple TV's Limitations

The tvOS and iOS are very similar, however, there are several differences and limitations:

- *Users can't tap their screens*: Users will find it frustrating using the remote to enter data into a tvOS app. They will likely experience this right away when entering user names and passwords. They may have to retype their entire password if they got distracted and forgot where they left off. Users will find it very helpful to pair a Bluetooth keyboard with their Apple TV when this feature becomes available.

- *No persistent local storage*: tvOS offers no persistent local storage. The lack of local storage means any app maker must use CloudKit, Parse, or some other cloud-based service to save files or any other significant amount of information within their app.

- *Developers can only access 500KB of persistent storage*. This is what is local to the device to save basic app settings and configuration information using the NSUserDefaults class. *Only the temporary and cache directories can be written to.* The standard documents directory is not accessible.

- *There is a 200MB app size limit*: tvOS enforces a 200MB limit on the size of each app. This will affect a number of apps, especially games. Game apps can easily reach 1GB due to the inclusion of graphic assets. Apps will have to use App Thinning and On-Demand Recourses to download additional assets when needed to address this restriction.

- *No web views*: This is probably the most drastic restriction that developers are going to have to work with; especially for apps that are mostly web views. Apple does offer an alternative in the form of TVML. This enables developers to define their views to create a client-server app with the TVJS JavaScript APIs. This also means it will be more difficult to view Word documents and PDFs that were easily viewable in UIWebviews with iOS.

- *No built-in PiP*. Picture-in-Picture was introduced in iOS 9 but is not available with tvOS.

- *No customizable video player*: The built-in video player in AVKit for tvOS does not support the ability to extend customizations.

- *No photos access*: tvOS does support viewing photos stored in iCloud, but developers don't have the ability to display the photo picker via UIKit's UIImagePickerController or the Photos framework.

- *No address book, calendar, or iMessage*: Apps will not be able to incorporate the Address Book, Contacts, or EventKit frameworks. The MessagesUI framework also isn't available, making it impossible to send iMessages.

- *No ReplayKit*: ReplayKit is targeted at game developers and lets players record their gameplay to share with other players online. It is possible the reason for this omission is that the Apple TV isn't powerful enough to record 1080p gameplay while rendering the actual game.

- *No Pasteboard API*: Pasteboard enables copy and paste functionality on iOS but it is not available for tvOS.

- *No multipeer connectivity*: The multipeer connectivity framework handles identifying iOS devices via Wi-Fi, peer-to-peer Wi-Fi, and Bluetooth, and then managing the transfer of data between devices.

- *No Mach Messages and Named Pipes*: Mach Messages and Named Pipes are low-level kernel technologies that enable interprocess communications. This enables processes to pass messages to each other.

Advantages with tvOS Development

The Apple TV and tvOS are new, and that brings several advantages over iOS development, at least for now:

- You only need to develop for a single screen resolution.

- There is no need to handle screen rotations or size class changes.

- Unlike mobile cell phones and tablets, tvOS developers can assume the presence of low-latency, always on, high-bandwidth networks.

Some Notes About Developing in Swift with tvOS

When the Apple TV and tvOS were introduced, the Swift programming language had been available for over a year. We had each been using Objective-C for over six years, but immediately started using Swift for new app development. We will be using Swift in this book.

Although we love developing in Swift, we feel there are a few caveats about Swift we must disclose.

Swift Pain Points

The Swift language is changing and changing fast. Some releases of Swift cause compiler errors in code that worked just fine in the previous Swift version. Although the changes are usually minimal and improve the language, the compiler errors still take time to fix.

Developer tools are still lagging behind Objective-C. Sometimes the debugger refuses to disclose variable results, and compiler errors can be vague or misleading. It's hard to believe that a year and a half since the introduction of Swift the Refactor command in Xcode still does not work!

Compiler stability can be an issue. Sometimes Xcode will crash, and heavy use of Swift frameworks sometimes don't work well with "whole module optimization."

Swift Advantages

Swift may not be completely mature yet, but it is ready for prime time. It is a pleasure to code in Swift and we have noticed about a third of the code you would have to write in Objective-C is no longer necessary in Swift. For example, Interface Sections are no longer necessary in Swift.

Swift does fulfill the promise of more efficient and modern development. An entire class of errors that used to require runtime debugging are now caught by the compiler. We spend about a quarter of the time debugging Swift apps than we would have with Objective-C.

The tvOS Focus Engine

Interactions in tvOS present a unique challenge to developers and user interface designers. The new Apple TV pairs a remote and a potential wireless game controller with a user interface that lacks a traditional cursor. This results in "focus" being the only way an app can provide visual feedback to users as they navigate within the app.

The focus engine can be thought of as a bridgekeeper between users and your tvOS application. Understanding the focus engine is an essential step toward building an app that feels native to tvOS, and not just a quick, ugly iOS port.

Every experienced iOS developer will feel comfortable with UIKit and tvOS, and Apple has made it easy to port your iOS app to tvOS. However, if you don't consider how your app needs to interact with the focus engine from the start, you will find yourself frustrated with the user interaction as you finish your app.

What Does Focusable Mean?

Users navigate a tvOS application by moving focus between user interface (UI) items on their TVs. When a UI item is focused, its appearance is adjusted to stand out from the appearance of other items. Focus effects are what make the new Apple TV and tvOS communal. Focus effects provide visual feedback not only to whoever is using the remote, but also to friends and family who may be watching. This is what separates the native tvOS experience from AirPlaying your iPhone or iPad app onto the TV.

Only one view can be in focus at a time, and only views can receive focus. Consider the buttons in Figure 1-3.

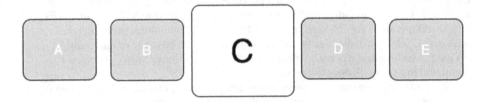

tvOS Views or Buttons

Figure 1-3. Button C is focusable

Button C is currently in focus. Swiping left of the Apple TV remote will focus button B. Swiping right on the Apple TV remote will focus button D. Swiping left or right more aggressively will focus button A or button E, respectively.

Apple has updated UIKit and provided implementations for views that can become focusable by providing a method called `canBecomeFocused()`.

Only the following UIKit classes can become focused:

- UIButton

- UIControl

- UISegmentedControl

- UITabBar

- UITextField

- UISearchBar

Summary

The new Apple TV offers a great opportunity for developers. The tools that are available in tvOS enable developers to deploy a new generation of apps on a new device in users' homes.

Exercises

1. Read the Human Interface Guidelines for tvOS. You can read the HIG for tvOS at `https://developer.apple.com/tvos/human-interface-guidelines/`.

2. If you haven't already registered for a developer account, go register! You can register at `https://developer.apple.com`.

CHAPTER 2

▪ ▪ ▪

The tvOS Weather App

This chapter will show you the capabilities of the tvOS by walking you through the steps on how to create a basic tvOS weather app. The app will demonstrate how UIKit controls look differently on tvOS than they do on iOS and how the development process is nearly identical. You will use this weather app for both this chapter and Chapter 3. In Chapter 3 you will use Stack Views to lay out part of this weather app.

Building this weather app will also enable you to explore how the focus engine works and how you can use it in your apps. The goal of the weather app will be to look up the current weather in different cities using www.OpenWeatherMap.org, a free web service (see Figure 2-1).

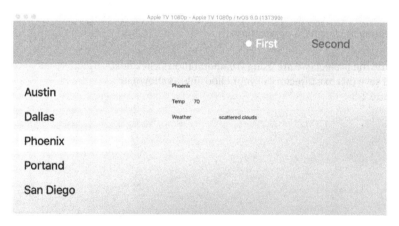

Figure 2-1. *The weather app you will develop including UITabBarController, UITableView, and UIStackViews*

The cool thing about tvOS development is how similar it's to iOS development. Let's start building this weather app by choosing a template for the app based on the Tabbed Application and include a Table View and labels.

1. Create a new tvOS Xcode project and select Tabbed Application. Then click Next (see Figure 2-2).

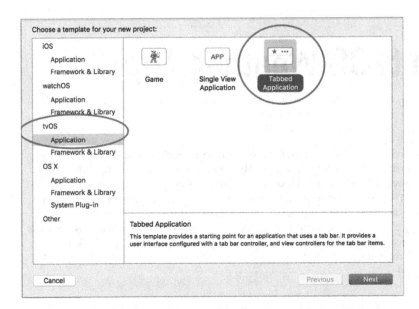

Figure 2-2. *Creating the first tvOS application*

2. Name the project (we are using WeatherStation), click next, and save this to a directory of your choosing, as shown in Figure 2-3.

Choose options for your new project:

Product Name:	WeatherStation
Organization Name:	xcelMe
Organization Identifier:	com
Bundle Identifier:	com.WeatherStation
Language:	Swift

✓ Include Unit Tests
✓ Include UI Tests

Cancel   Previous   Next

Figure 2-3. *Naming and saving the WeatherStation app*

When the project is created, the project settings are displayed, as shown in Figure 2-4.

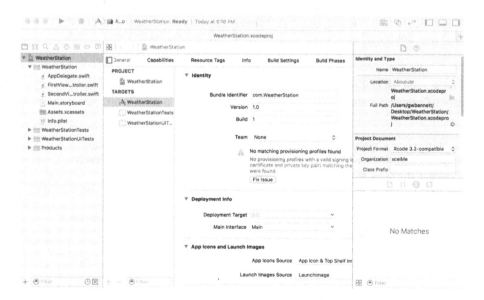

Figure 2-4. *The WeatherStation app project settings*

As shown in Figure 2-4, `FirstViewController.swift` and `SecondViewController.swift` files are created, one for each tab.

3. Click the Main.Storyboard file and view the Storyboard in Interface Builder, as shown in Figure 2-5.

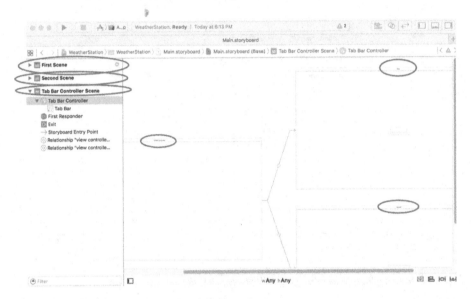

Figure 2-5. *The WeatherStation app Storyboard*

When the storyboard file is shown, you can see there are three scenes. The UITabBarController acts as the entry point to the application and also serves as the RootViewController that contains the First Scene and Second Scene View Controllers.

■ **Note** You will frequently need to zoom in and out in the Storyboard to see all the scenes. Command + and Command − will quickly enable you to zoom in and out.

We created a Tabbed Application with two tabs to demonstrate how many of the UIKit controls look and behave differently in tvOS compared to iOS. You will be working in the Main.storyboard file and the FirstViewController.swift file. You will not be working with the `SecondViewController.swift` file directly; but you will be using the `SecondViewController.swift` file for our exercises at the end of this chapter.

Let's run the WeatherStation app to see what it looks like in the tvOS simulator (see Figure 2-6). Click the Play button to run the WeatherStation app.

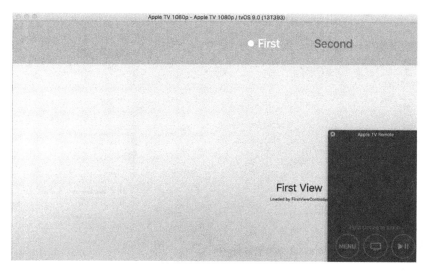

Figure 2-6. *The WeatherStation app running in the tvOS Simulator with the remote in the lower right hand corner*

You can see that the Tab Bar is at the top of the view in tvOS instead of the bottom of the view as in iOS apps. Use the remote to switch between tabs and dismiss the Tab Bar by swiping.

■ **Note** If you are not able to view the remote, you can access it by going to the tvOS Simulator menu and selecting Hardware ➤ Show Apple TV Remote or entering Shift-Command-R.

Designing the View

Now let's add the Table View and Label controls to the First Scene.

4.   Select the Main.storyboard file and select the First Scene.

5.   Remove the two labels in the middle of the First Scene (see Figure 2-7).

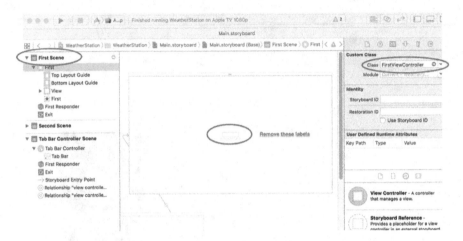

Figure 2-7. *Removing the Labels in the First Scene*

6. Add a Table View to the First Scene and five Labels, as shown in Figure 2-8.

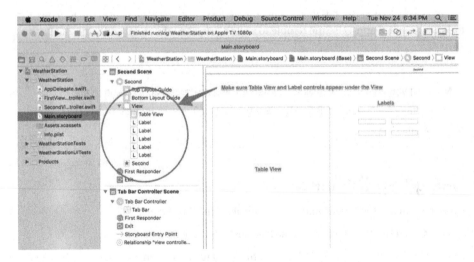

Figure 2-8. *Adding UI Controls to the First Scene*

■ **Note** You will need to expand your scene to 100% in Interface Builder to add your Table View and Labels. Make sure the controls appear under the Document Outline Section in Interface Builder. (see Figure 2-8).

7. Add and connect the outlets to the controls, as shown in Figure 2-9.

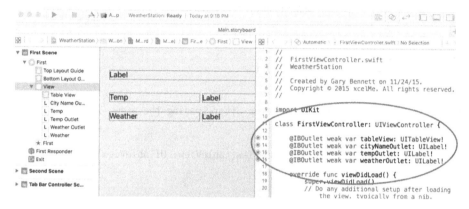

Figure 2-9. *Connect the control outlets*

8. Connect the dataSource and delegate outlets for the Table View, as shown in Figure 2-10.

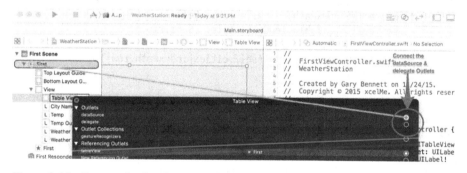

Figure 2-10. *Connect the dataSource and delegate outlets*

Adding the Code for the View

Now let's add the additional code to populate the Table View by adding the code in Listing 2-1.

Listing 2-1. Code to Populate the Table View

```
13    @IBOutlet weak var tableView: UITableView!
14    @IBOutlet weak var cityNameOutlet: UILabel!
15    @IBOutlet weak var tempOutlet: UILabel!
16    @IBOutlet weak var weatherOutlet: UILabel!
17
18    var cities = ["Austin","Dallas","Phoenix", "Portand", "San Diego"]
19
20    override func viewDidLoad() {
21        super.viewDidLoad()
22
23        // Do any additional setup after loading the view.
24    }
25
26    func numberOfSectionsInTableView(tableView: UITableView) -> Int {
27        return 1
28    }
29
30    func tableView(tableView: UITableView, numberOfRowsInSection section:
      Int) -> Int {
31        return self.cities.count
32    }
33
34    func tableView(tableView: UITableView, cellForRowAtIndexPath
      indexPath: NSIndexPath) -> UITableViewCell {
35        let cell = UITableViewCell(style: .Subtitle,
           reuseIdentifier: nil)
36        cell.textLabel?.text = (self.cities[indexPath.row])
37        return cell
38    }
```

Line 18 contains the array of the cities for which you want to display the weather information.

Lines 30 to 40 contain the data source and delegate functions to populate the Table View.

Now run the app in the tvOS simulator to see the city names appear in the Table View. Practice using the remote in the simulator to change the focus in between cities (see Figure 2-11).

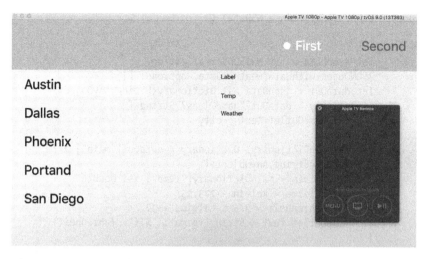

Figure 2-11. *Running the app with the Table View being populated*

Now let's retrieve the weather information from www.OpenWeatherMap.org. Insert the code as shown in Listing 2-2.

Listing 2-2. Codeto Retrieve Weather Information

```
41 func tableView(tableView: UITableView, didSelectRowAtIndexPath indexPath:
   NSIndexPath) {
42        let row = indexPath.row
43        self.getWeatherData(cities[row])
44    }
45
46    func getWeatherData(city: String){
47        let urlString: String = city.
          stringByAddingPercentEncodingWithAllowedCharacters
          (NSCharacterSet.URLQueryAllowedCharacterSet())!
48        //PLEASE VISIT http://home.openweathermap.org/users/sign_up to
          get your API Key. Insert your API key below
49        let url = NSURL(string: "http://api.openweathermap.org/data/2.5/
          weather?q=\(urlString),us&APPID=INSERT YOUR API KEY HERE")
50        let getData = NSURLSession.sharedSession().dataTaskWithURL(url!)
          {(data,response,error ) in
51           dispatch_async(dispatch_get_main_queue(), {
52              self.setLables(data!)
53           })
54        }
55        getData.resume()
56    }
57
```

```
58      func setLables(weatherData:NSData) {
59
60          do {
61              let jsonData = try NSJSONSerialization.
                JSONObjectWithData(weatherData, options: [])
62              let dataOut = jsonData as! Dictionary<String,AnyObject>
63              if let city = dataOut["name"] as? String {
64                  cityNameOutlet.text = city
65              }
66              if let mainDictionary: Dictionary = dataOut["main"] as?
                Dictionary<String,AnyObject>{
67                  let kelvin = mainDictionary["temp"] as! Double
68                  let celsius = kelvin - 273.15
69                  let fahrenheit = 9/5 * celsius + 32
70                  tempOutlet.text = String(format: "%.f", fahrenheit)
71              }
72
73              if let weatherDict = dataOut["weather"]![0]{
74                  weatherOutlet.text = weatherDict["description"] as?
                    String
75
76              }
77          }
78          catch {
79              print("Fetch failed:")
80          }
81      }
```

Lines 41 to 44 contain the didSelectRowAtIndexPath delegate method. This method gets called when the user has selected a city. This method retrieves the row that was selected and then calls the function getWeatherData with the name of the city that was selected.

Lines 46 to 56 contain the getWeatherData function. Line 47 takes the city string that was passed in and replaces any spaces in the name (San Diego) with %20 (San%20Diego).

Line 49 then creates the URL used to request the weather data for the city. The URL String for the city is passed into the URL and the API key is used by OpenWeatherMap.org functions as a parameter at the end of the string.

Lines 50 to 55 make an asynchronous request to OpenWeatherMap.org to retrieve the weather information for the selected city. When the weather data are successfully downloaded, Line 52 calls setLables and passes the weather data that was downloaded for the selected city.

Lines 58 to 81 convert the data downloaded to JSON and parses them to retrieve the city name, temperature, and description of the weather.

Lines 61 and 62 convert the NSData to a JSON dictionary.

Lines 63 and 64 then look up the name of the city and set the cityNameOutlet text outlet.

Lines 66 and 67 look up the temperature data. OpenWeatherMap.org returns temperatures in Kelvin.

Lines 68 to 70 convert Kelvin to Celsius and then to Fahrenheit. The temperature is then sent to the weatherOutlet text outlet.

Now run the app to test that the weather data have updated with the city that was selected.

When you run the app, it will crash on line 52, self.setLables(data!). Starting with iOS 9, Apple has enforced using secure connections with websites. Because OpenWeatherMap.com is not a secure SSL connection (i.e., one that uses https://), Apple blocks the web service request. You can see what happened in the Output console, as shown in Figure 2-12.

Figure 2-12. *iOS 9 blocking nonsecure (without https://) web service requests*

White Listing Websites

As Apple indicates in the Console, you can configure your Info.plist file to enable only this website's address to be accessed without it being an TLS URL. This is called *white listing*. To white list a website, you will need to modify the Info.plist.

1. Right-click the Info.plist in the Project Navigator. Then Select Open As ➤ Source Code, as shown in Figure 2-13.

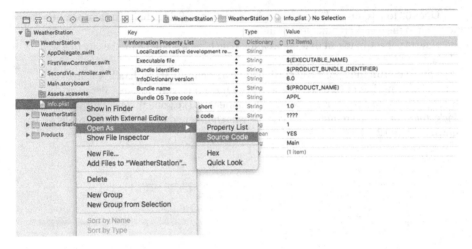

Figure 2-13. *Opening the apps Info.Plist*

2. Add the code in Listing 2-3 to the Info.plist starting at line 31. The file should then appear as shown in Figure 2-14.

Listing 2-3. Info.plist

```
31 <key>NSAppTransportSecurity</key>
32 <dict>
33   <key>NSExceptionDomains</key>
34   <dict>
35     <key>api.openweathermap.org</key>
36     <dict>
37       <!--Include to allow subdomains-->
38       <key>NSIncludesSubdomains</key>
39       <true/>
40       <!--Include to allow HTTP requests-->
41       <key>NSTemporaryExceptionAllowsInsecureHTTPLoads</key>
42       <true/>
43       <!--Include to specify minimum TLS version-->
44       <key>NSTemporaryExceptionMinimumTLSVersion</key>
45       <string>TLSv1.1</string>
46     </dict>
47   </dict>
48 </dict>
```

```
                                    Info.plist
 🔲  <  >  🔖 WeatherStation ⟩ 🔖 WeatherStation ⟩ 🔖 Info.plist ⟩ 🔖 <dict>
18        <string>1.0</string>
19      <key>CFBundleSignature</key>
20      <string>????</string>
21      <key>CFBundleVersion</key>
22      <string>1</string>
23      <key>LSRequiresIPhoneOS</key>
24      <true/>
25      <key>UIMainStoryboardFile</key>
26      <string>Main</string>
27      <key>UIRequiredDeviceCapabilities</key>
28      <array>
29          <string>arm64</string>
30      </array>
31      <key>NSAppTransportSecurity</key>
32      <dict>
33          <key>NSExceptionDomains</key>
34          <dict>
35              <key>api.openweathermap.org</key>
36              <dict>
37                  <!--Include to allow subdomains-->
38                  <key>NSIncludesSubdomains</key>
39                  <true/>
40                  <!--Include to allow HTTP requests-->
41                  <key>NSTemporaryExceptionAllowsInsecureHTTPLoads</key>
42                  <true/>
43                  <!--Include to specify minimum TLS version-->
44                  <key>NSTemporaryExceptionMinimumTLSVersion</key>
45                  <string>TLSv1.1</string>
46              </dict>
47          </dict>
48      </dict>
49
50
51  </dict>
52  </plist>
53
```

Figure 2-14. *Updated Info.plist source code*

3. Close the Info.plist file and open it by clicking it. The Info.plist should appear as shown in Figure 2-15.

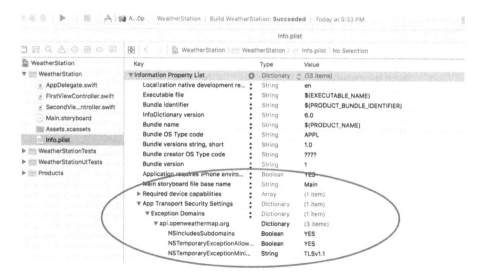

Figure 2-15. *Updated Info.plist*

Now that you have white listed the OpenWeatherMap.org website, you can run the app and retrieve the weather data for selected cities. Run the app and test the selecting of cities. The weather data should populate, as shown in Figure 2-16.

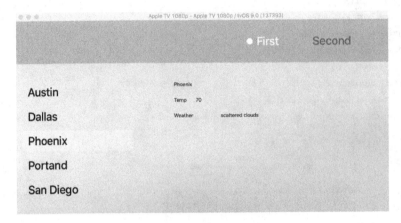

Figure 2-16. App running and retrieving weather data

Summary

In this chapter you learned how to develop a basic and functional tvOS app. You learned how to retrieve data from a web service and display it and learned how to white list a website.

In the next chapter we will use Stack Views layout our labels and explore the tvOS Focus Engine.

Exercises

1. Read the OpenWeatherMap.org API JSON format and add the ability to display humidity, barometric pressure, and wind direction to the view.

2. In the Second Scene, display an icon of the current weather that the selected city is experiencing. For example, if it is snowing, display a snowflake.

■ ■ ■

CHAPTER 3

Stack Views and the Focus Engine

In iOS 9 Apple introduced Stack Views, and these are also available in tvOS. The UIStackView class provides an interface for laying out collections of views in either a column or a row. A Stack View lets you utilize Auto Layout, creating user interfaces that can dynamically adapt to any changes in the available space within your views. In iOS 9 Stack Views automatically adjust for autorotation and screen size.

In this chapter we will expand our WeatherStation app to use Stack Views and also explore how the tvOS Focus Engine works.

Auto Layout and Stack Views

Stack View uses Auto Layout to position and size its views. The Stack View will pin the first and last arranged view flush with its edge along the stack's axis. When working with a horizontal stack, this means the first arranged view's leading edge is pinned to the stack's leading edge, and the last arranged view's trailing edge is pinned to the stack's trailing edge. When working with vertical stacks, the top and bottom edges are pinned, respectively. You will see this in action in our example below.

You can then specify how you want the spacing to appear between the views in a stack, all without having to specify the constraints in a stack.

Implementing Stacks

Implementing stacks is pretty easy. The steps below will show how to embed five labels into a single stack.

1. Open the WeatherStation app from the previous chapter.

2. Select the City Name Label.

3. At the bottom right of Interface Builder, click the Stack icon.

4. Ensure that the Stack View Axis that Interface Builder selected is set to "Vertical" as shown in Figure 3-1.

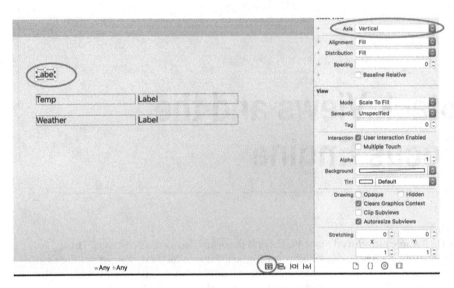

Figure 3-1. *Placing the City Name label in a Vertical Stack View*

5. Select both Temperature Labels.

6. At the bottom right of Interface Builder, click the Stack icon.

7. Ensure that the Stack View Axis that Interface Builder selected is set to "Horizontal," as shown in Figure 3-2.

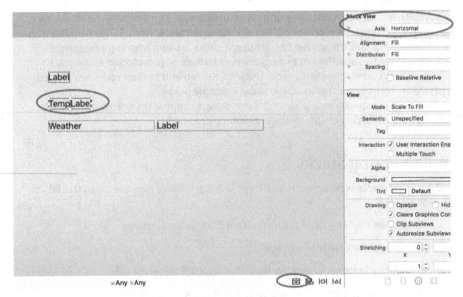

Figure 3-2. *Placing the Temp labels in a horizontal Stack View*

24

You will notice that Interface Builder is smart about choosing the correct Axis settings when selecting multiple controls.

8. Select both bottom Weather Labels.

9. At the bottom right of the Interface Builder, click the Stack icon.

10. Ensure that the Stack View Axis that Interface Builder selected is set to "Horizontal," as shown in Figure 3-3.

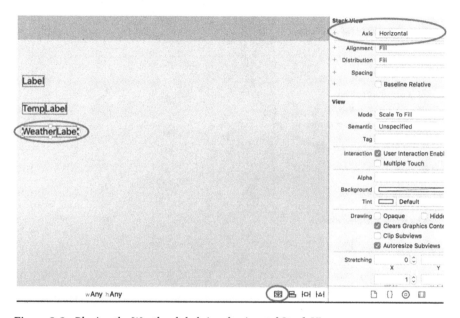

Figure 3-3. *Placing the Weather labels in a horizontal Stack View*

You should see all five labels in three different Stack Views, as shown in Figure 3-4.

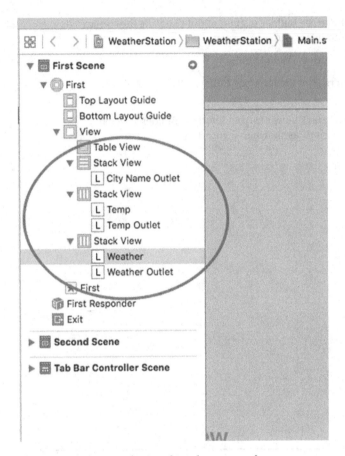

Figure 3-4. *Three Stack Views have been created*

11. Now select all three Stack Views and click the Stack icon to
    embed these stacks into one stack, as shown in Figure 3-5.

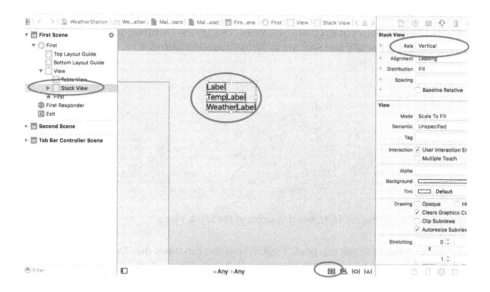

Figure 3-5. One Vertical Stack View created from the three Stack Views

> ■ **Note** Xcode 7.1.1 Issue: When completing Step 11 above, the labels may not look as they do in Figure 3-5 and Figure 3-6. Simply select another file and then select the Main. storyboard file. This will cause Xcode to reset the view correctly.

Ensure the Stack View is a Vertical Axis Stack View. This makes all the views in the Stack View alignment based vertically to one another.

It appears that all the labels are crunched together. Let's improve the spacing in the one Stack View.

12. Click the parent Stack View, then change the Distribution to Fill Equally and spacing to 30, as shown in Figure 3-6.

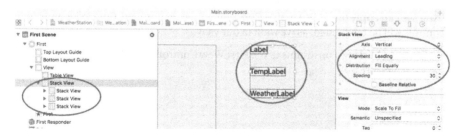

Figure 3-6. Increasing the Vertical Spacing of the Stack Views

13. To increase the horizontal spacing of the Temp and Weather labels, select both child Stack Views, change the Distribution to Fill Equally and Spacing to 30, as shown in Figure 3-7.

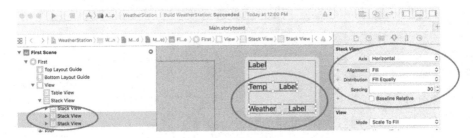

Figure 3-7. Increasing the Horizontal Spacing of the Stack Views

Now that you have the one parent Stack View, you can unset the "Extend Edges Under Top Bars" and Add Missing Constraints in 2 steps. This will enable the First View to shift automatically scroll up and down when the Tab Bar is visible.

14. Select the First View Controller and uncheck Extend Edges – Under Top Bars, as shown in Figure 3-8.

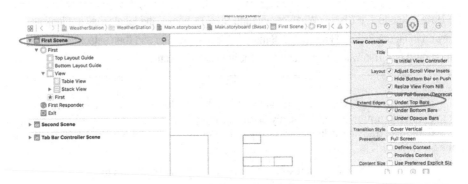

Figure 3-8. Uncheck Extend Edges – Under Top Bars

Now we can apply the "Add Missing Constraints" tool to our View Controller and all our controls will be positioned, as we want in our view.

15. Add Missing Constraints to the First View Controller, as shown in Figure 3-9.

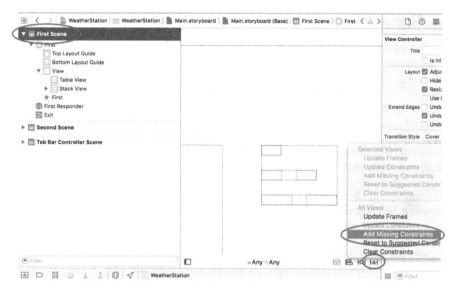

Figure 3-9. *Adding Missing Constraints to our First Scene*

Congratulations! You did it. Run the app now so you can see how the two constraints for the Stack View place all five labels where you want them. More importantly, if you add other controls to the view, you only need to update the constraints for the parent stack, not all five labels (see Figure 3-10).

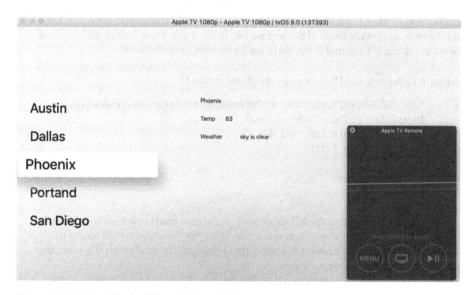

Figure 3-10. *The Weather App with Stack Views*

The Focus Engine

With tvOS there are no tap or touch gestures, instead Apple provides the Focus Engine.

According to Apple, "the process within the UIKit that controls focus and focus movement is called the focus engine. The user controls focus through the remote and game controllers. The focus engine listens for incoming focus-movement events from all these input devices. When an event comes in, it automatically determines where focus should update and notifies the app. This system helps to create a consistent user experience across apps, provides automatic support for all current and future input methods in every app, and helps developers concentrate on implementing their app's unique behavior rather than defining or reinventing basic navigation. Only the focus engine can update focus. There is no API for directly setting the focused view or moving focus in a certain direction. The focus engine only updates focus if the user sends a movement event, if the system requests an update, or if the application requests an update."

The great thing about the focus engine is that it looks at the interface layout and handles all the work when moving the focus from one item to another.

There are many new functions and properties available to control the way focus is handled within tvOS apps. Many of these are defined by the UIFocusEnvironment protocol, which the UIViewController, UIView, UIWindow, and UIPresentationController classes automatically conform to. There are also several methods contained in the UITableViewDelegate and UICollectionViewDelegate protocols that can be used to control the focus within your app.

A Focus Engine Example

Let's say you wanted to skip focus for one of the cities in our weather app as the user scrolls through the city list with their remote. You could add some code to do this. Let's add the code to skip the focus of the second city in the Table View, Dallas. Add the code as shown in Listing 3-1 starting at line 58 in the FirstViewController.swift.

Listing 3-1. Adding :canFocusRowAtIndexPath: method

```
58    func tableView(tableView: UITableView, canFocusRowAtIndexPath
      indexPath: NSIndexPath) -> Bool {
59        if indexPath.row == 1 {
60            return false
61        }
62        return true
63    }
```

Here you implemented the UItableView(_:canFocusRowAtIndexPath:) method to return false when the indexPath.row is equal to 1. Otherwise you would return true. The UItableView(_:canFocusRowAtIndexPath:) delegate method determines whether specific rows can be can obtain focus.

When you run the app now, you'll notice that when you try to navigate the rows in the Table View, the Dallas row is skipped because you implemented the UItableView(_:canFocusRowAtIndexPath:) method.

Summary

In this chapter you learned how Stack Views and the focus engine work. Stack Views are available in iOS and tvOS, but the focus engine is only available in tvOS. The Focus Engine is available only for tvOS because we can't tap on our TVs.

Stack Views can save lots of time during the development lifecycle of an app. Understanding the focus engine will enable you to add to the user's interface experience as you create your tvOS applications.

In the next few chapters, we will be exploring some of the more common Apple TV user interface elements while building a Photo Gallery application.

Exercises

1. Modify the Stack Views so the Temp and Weather labels are aligned and laid out more consistently.

2. Add Constraints within the Stack Views for better readability.

3. Disable more than one city in the Table View.

4. Add a button to the First Scene and make the button have focus when the app starts. The button doesn't need to do anything, other than just have focus when the app starts.

CHAPTER 4

■ ■ ■

Creating a Photo Gallery App

For the next few chapters, we will be exploring some of the more common Apple TV user interface elements while building a Photo Gallery application. Most of the user interface elements will be familiar to you if you are an experienced iOS developer, but the way that the user interacts with them is somewhat different since you cannot walk up to your television and start tapping and swiping on the screen. (Not yet, anyway!)

Page View Controllers

The first user interface element that you will be exploring is the Page View Controller. The Page View Controller consists of a number of full-screen views that the user navigates through by swiping left or right between them. A common component of the Page View Controller is the Page Control, which is a series of horizontal white dots along the bottom of the views to indicate both the number of pages available as well as which page the user is currently viewing. An example of a Page View Controller containing a number of full-screen images is shown in Figure 4-1.

Figure 4-1. *An example of a Page View Controller and its associated Page Control*

From the Page Control near the bottom, you can see that there are five pages in this Page View Controller, and the user is currently looking at page number three.

For the Photo Gallery app, you are going to create an app consisting primarily of a Page View Controller that will present the user with a series of full-screen Image View pages. With each page containing a different photo, this will really take advantage of the full 1080p high-definition screen available to an Apple TV app.

Creating the Photo Gallery App

1. To get started creating the Photo Gallery app, open Xcode and select File ➤ New ➤ Project.

2. Next, choose Application under tvOS, then Single View Application, as shown in Figure 4-2.

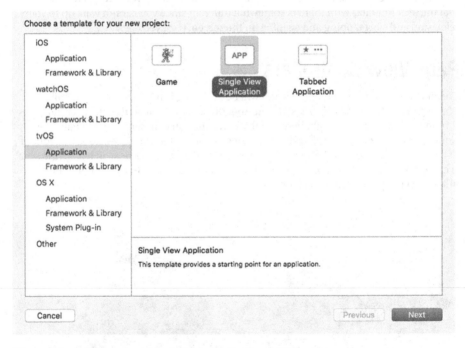

Figure 4-2. *Creating a new Single View Application tvOS project*

3. After clicking Next, enter Photo Gallery for the Product Name and choose Swift for the Language, as shown in Figure 4-3.

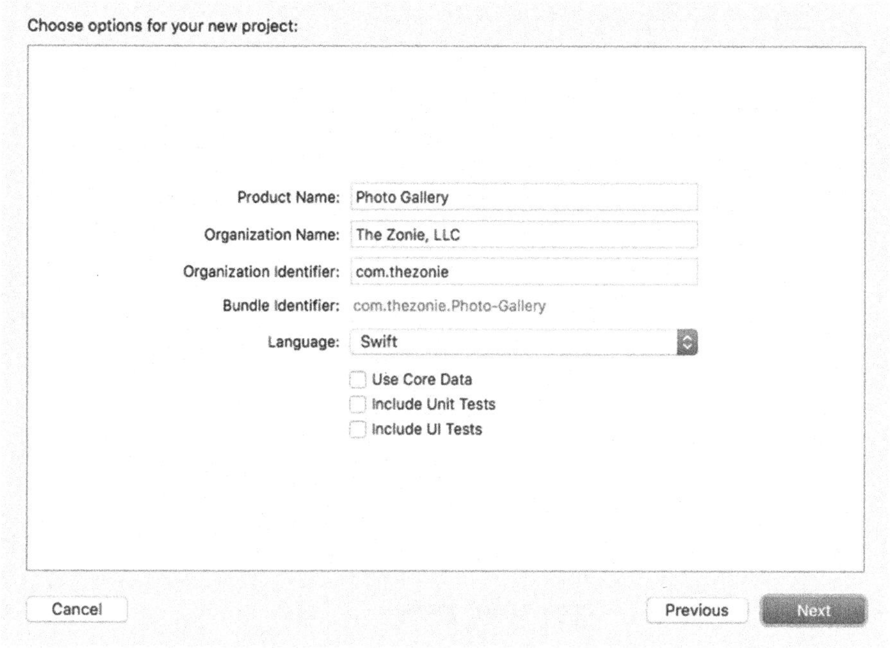

Choose options for your new project:

Product Name: Photo Gallery

Organization Name: The Zonie, LLC

Organization Identifier: com.thezonie

Bundle Identifier: com.thezonie.Photo-Gallery

Language: Swift

☐ Use Core Data
☐ Include Unit Tests
☐ Include UI Tests

Cancel   Previous   Next

Figure 4-3. *Creating the Photo Gallery Project*

4.   Click Next again and choose a location (for example, your
      Desktop or Documents folder) where you would like to save
      the project, then click Create.

You should now be looking at your newly created Photo Gallery project, as shown in
Figure 4-4.

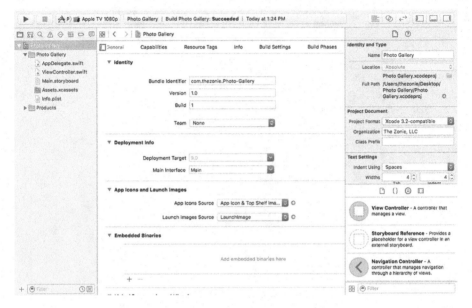

Figure 4-4. *The newly created Photo Gallery project*

A Little Project Cleanup

Now that you have created your project, you first have to do a little cleanup. Since this app will be built around a Page View Controller, you don't need the default View Controller that was created with the project.

1. To remove the default View Controller, first right-click (or Control-click) the ViewController.swift file in the Project navigator and select Delete, as shown in Figure 4-5, followed by Move to Trash when prompted.

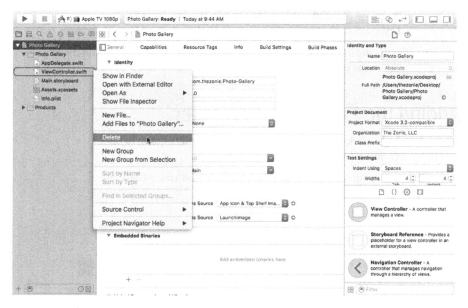

Figure 4-5. *Removing the default View Controller*

2. Next, you need to select the Main.storyboard file and then
    select the View Controller scene as shown in Figure 4-6.

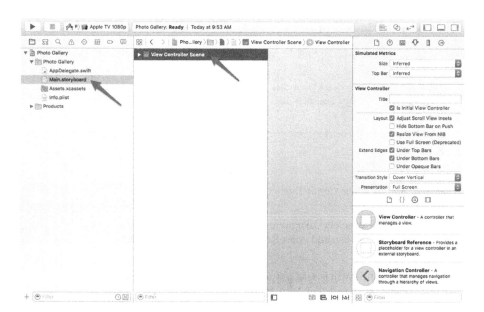

Figure 4-6. *Selecting the View Controller scene*

3. To delete the scene, either press the Delete key on your keyboard or choose Edit ➤ Delete from the application menu.

Now that the default View Controller has been removed, it is time to add the Page View Controller to the project.

Adding the Page View Controller

1. Right-click (or Control-click) the Photo Gallery group in the Project navigator and select New File.

2. Select Source under tvOS, then select Cocoa Touch Class, as shown in Figure 4-7.

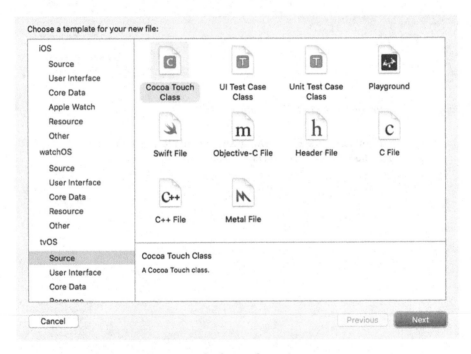

Figure 4-7. Adding a new Cocoa Touch Class to the project

3. Click Next, select UIPageViewController from the Subclass drop-down list, and enter PageViewController as the Class name.

4. Make sure Swift is selected as the Language (as shown in Figure 4-8), and click Next, followed by Create to add it to the project.

Choose options for your new file:

Class: PageViewController

Subclass of: UIPageViewController

☐ Also create XIB file

Language: Swift

Cancel   Previous   Next

Figure 4-8. *Adding the new PageViewController class to the project*

Now that you have added the PageViewController class, you need to add a Page Content View Controller to the project to handle displaying the pages of images from within the Page View Controller itself.

1. Right-click (or Control-click) the Photo Gallery group in the Project navigator to add another New File to the project, but this time, select UIViewController from the Subclass drop-down list and name the class PageContentViewController.

Adding Scenes to the Interface Builder Canvas

Now that you have added the PageViewController and PageContentViewController classes to the project, the next step is to add the associated scenes to the Main.storyboard file and associate them with your two new classes.

1. First, select the Main.storyboard file from the Project navigator to view its empty canvas.

2. Select the Object library in the Utilities area of Xcode and drag a Page View Controller onto the canvas.

3. Select the Page View Controller and choose the Attributes inspector from the Utilities area and check the Is Initial View Controller check box (as shown in Figure 4-9) to indicate that this is the first view controller that will be loaded when the app is launched.

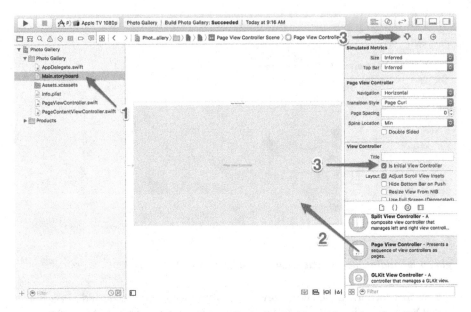

Figure 4-9. Adding a new Page View Controller to the Main.storyboard and setting it as the Initial View Controller

---

■ **Note**   In tvOS, the scenes within a storyboard are large, each the size of a full 1080p television screen. This can make it difficult to navigate a storyboard containing multiple scenes. To remedy this, you can zoom in and out of a storyboard by pressing Command + and Command –, respectively.

---

4. Next, select Scroll from the Transition Style drop-down list instead of Page Curl (as shown in Figure 4-10) to cause the Page View Controller to show the Page Control with its horizontal white dots, as shown previously in Figure 4-1.

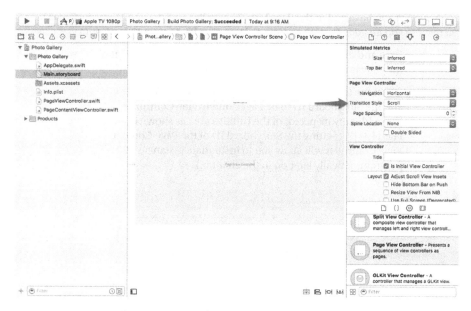

Figure 4-10. *Setting the Transition Style to Scroll*

5. Finally, with the Page View Controller scene still selected, select the Identity inspector in the Utilities area and set the Class to PageViewController, as shown in Figure 4-11.

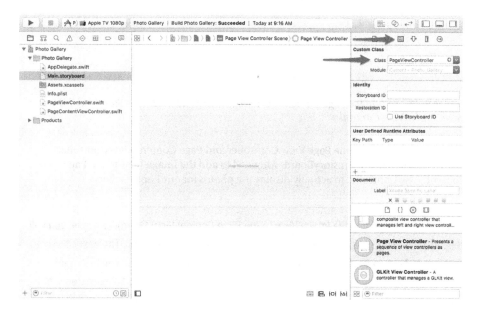

Figure 4-11. *Setting the Page View Controller scene class to PageViewController*

Now that you have added the Page View Controller scene to the Main.storyboard, you need to add an additional View Controller for the PageContentViewController class.

1. Drag and drop a View Controller from the Object library onto the canvas underneath the Page View Controller scene.

2. Select the new View Controller and set both the Class and the Storyboard ID to be PageContentViewController in the Identity inspector of the Utilities area as shown in Figure 4-12. (Setting the Storyboard ID of the Page Content View Controller will allow you to instantiate instances of it programmatically later on in the chapter.)

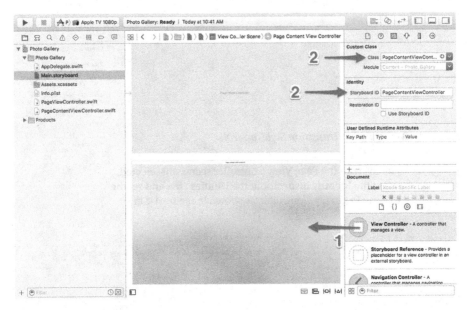

Figure 4-12. *Setting the Page Content View Controller scene class and Storyboard ID to PageContentViewController*

Now that you have the Page View Controller and Page Content View Controller scenes added to the Main.storyboard, you need to add the Image View to the Page Content View Controller to actually display the photos for our Photo Gallery.

■ **Note** Before adding the Image View to the Page Content View Controller scene, you will need to zoom back in again to 100% if you have previously zoomed out. The easiest way to do this is to hold down the Control and Command keys and press =. You can also right-click (or Control-click) anywhere on the empty blank space of the canvas and choose Zoom to 100%.

---

1. Drag and drop an Image View onto the Page Content View Controller scene, as shown in Figure 4-13.

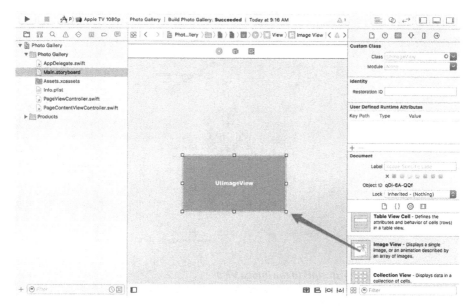

Figure 4-13. *Adding an Image View to the Page Content View Controller scene*

Since you are going to want the Image View to fill the entire screen, you will want to add some auto layout constraints to the Image View to pin it to the edges of the Page Content View Controller.

1. With the Image View selected, click the Pin Tool button in the layout bar at the bottom of the canvas.

2. Uncheck the Constrain to margins check box.

3. Select Items of New Constraints from the Update Frames drop-down list.

4. Add the four constraints shown in Figure 4-14.

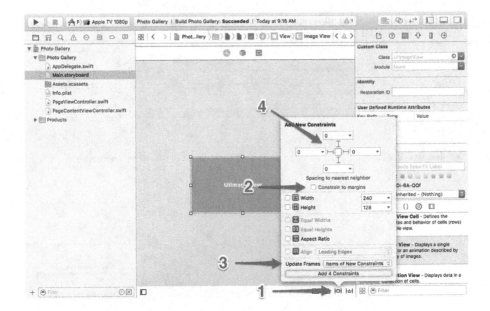

Figure 4-14. *Adding constraints to the Image View*

Now that the Image View fills the entire Page Content View Controller, the last thing you need to do is create an outlet for the Image View in the PageContentViewController. swift file.

1. Select the Page Content View Controller, and then click the Assistant editor icon ⟳ to also open the PageContentViewController.swift file, as shown in Figure 4-15.

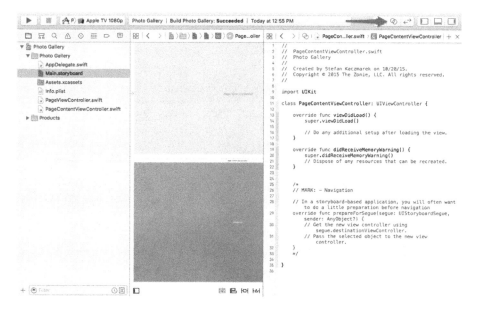

Figure 4-15. *Viewing the Page Content View Controller in the Assistant editor*

2. You may also want to hide the Utilities area temporarily by clicking the ⬚ button in the top-right corner of Xcode to give yourself more room to work.

3. Zoom the storyboard canvas back to 100% if zoomed out, and then right-click (or Control-click) and drag from the Image View to the first line within the PageContentViewController class definition to add a UIImageView outlet named imageView, as shown in Figure 4-16.

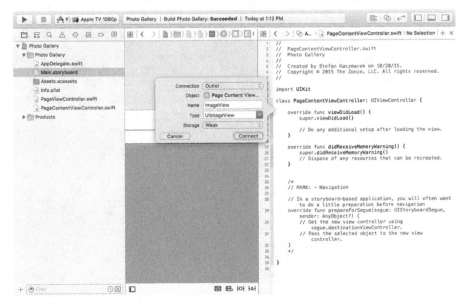

Figure 4-16. *Adding the* imageView *outlet to the* PageContentViewController *class*

Now that the Image View is connected to the imageView outlet, the scene work in Interface Builder is complete. You can now re-select the Standard editor (by clicking the ▦ icon in the top-right corner of Xcode) and turn your attention to adding the required data model structures to the project for the Photo Gallery app.

Adding the Photo and Album Data Model Structures

Since the purpose of a Photo Gallery app is to display a collection of photos, you are going to want to represent each of those photos using a custom data structure in order to keep things as clean and organized as possible. You are also going to create an Album structure to store a collection of related Photos. The completed app will allow the user to browse through an album of photos using the Page View Controller you have already created. So let's get started!

First, let's start by creating a Model group for these new structures under the Photo Gallery group in the Project navigator.

1. Right-click (or Control-click) the Photo Gallery group, select New Group, and name it Model.

2. Right-click (or Control-click) on the Model group and select New File.

3. Select Source under tvOS and then select Swift File.

4. Click Next and then name the file Photo.swift and then click Create.

Add the following code into the newly created Photo.swift file:

```
1    import Foundation
2
3    struct Photo {
4        var name: String = ""
5
6        init(name: String) {
7            self.name = name
8        }
9    }
```

This Swift Photo structure contains a single property, a String called name (Line 4), which will store the name of the photo associated with it.

Next, add another Swift File called Album.swift and add to it the code below:

```
1    import Foundation
2
3    struct Album {
4        var name: String = ""
5        var photos: [Photo] = []
6
7        init(name: String, photoNames: [String]) {
8            self.name = name
9            for photoName in photoNames {
10               self.photos += [Photo(name: photoName)]
11           }
12       }
13   }
```

The Album structure also contains a String name property (Line 4) as well as an array of Photo structures called photos (Line 5) that make up the contents of the album.

The Album structure also has a designated initializer (Line 7) that takes in the name of an album as well as an array of photo name Strings. The array of photo name Strings is then used to create the photos array of Photo structures when the Album is initialized (Lines 9-11).

Adding the Photo Image Files to the Asset Catalog

Now that you have created the Photo and Album data model structures, next you are going to add the actual photo image files to the project.

The best way to add images to an Xcode project is by adding them to an asset catalog. Asset catalogs simplify the organization and management of images in your app. When you created the Photo Gallery project, a default asset catalog named Assets.xcassets was created automatically.

1. To add the photo image files to the asset catalog, first click the Assets.xcassets folder in the Project navigator. By default, the Assets.xcassets contains an App Icon & Top Shelf Image folder, as well as a LaunchImage image, as shown in Figure 4-17.

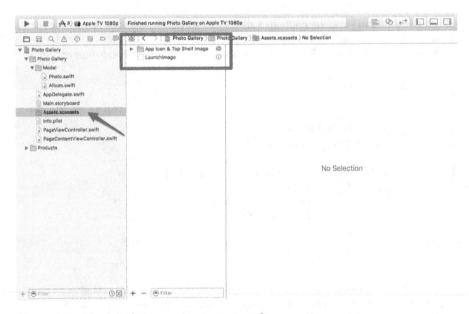

Figure 4-17. The default Assets.xcassets asset catalog

To add the photo image files to the asset catalog, first download the image files, as discussed in the Introduction to this book. After they have been downloaded and unzipped, simply drag and drop the Animals folder into the asset catalog set list, as shown in Figure 4-18.

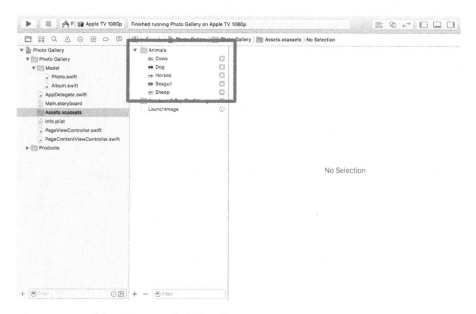

Figure 4-18. *Adding the Animals folder of images to the asset catalog*

Adding images to an asset catalog automatically copies the images to the project, so once they have been added, feel free to delete the original files you downloaded.

By default, when images are added to an asset catalog, they are added for All Universal devices, as shown in Figure 4-19. This means that a single image in an asset catalog can support multiple files at different resolutions (1x, 2x, 3x) for the various Apple devices available.

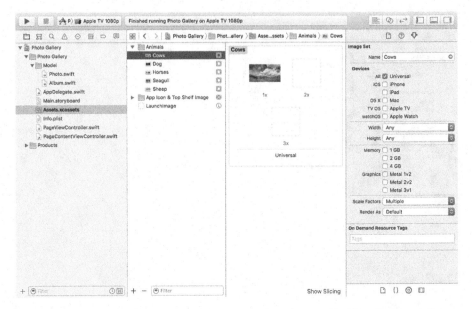

Figure 4-19. *By default, images added to an asset catalog are added for All Universal devices*

You don't need to support multiple resolutions as you are developing an Apple TV application, so for each of the images in the Animals folder, check the TV OS Apple TV check box, uncheck the All Universal check box, and then drag the image from the Unassigned spot to the 1x Apple TV spot, as shown in Figure 4-20.

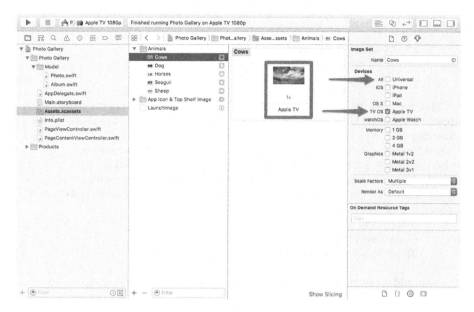

Figure 4-20. *Reassigning all of the Universal images to Apple TV images in the asset catalog*

Now that the photo image files have been added to the project, you can start filling in the details of the PageViewController and PageContentViewController classes. You are well on our way to finishing up this app!

Completing the Photo Gallery App

The only changes you have made to the PageContentViewController class up until this point was to add the UIImageView outlet earlier in the chapter. You still need to make a few more changes to complete the functionality of the Page Content View Controller.

After selecting the PageContentViewController.swift file from the Project navigator, add the following two lines to the beginning of the class definition:

```
1    var index: Int = 0
2    var photoName: String = ""
```

Since there will be multiple instantiations of the PageContentViewController class (one for each page in the Page View Controller), you will want each Page Content View Controller to keep track of both its page index (Line 1) and the name of its photo (Line 2). The Page View Controller will initialize these properties when it creates the Page Content View Controller.

Finally, add the following lines to the end of the viewDidLoad method:

```
1    if let image = UIImage(named: self.photoName) {
2        self.imageView.image = image
3    }
```

This initializes the Image View, loading in the photo represented by the photoName property that was set by the Page View Controller when it created the Page Content View Controller.

The final changes you need to make to complete the Photo Gallery app are within the main PageViewController class. Select the PageViewController.swift file in the Project navigator and have the PageViewController class adopt the UIPageViewControllerDataSource protocol by editing the first line of the class definition to match the following line of code:

```
1    class PageViewController: UIPageViewController,
     UIPageViewControllerDataSource {
```

Next, add the following properties at the beginning of the class definition:

```
1    var pageIndex: Int = 0
2    var album = Album(name: "Animals",
3              photoNames: ["Cows", "Dog",
4                      "Horses", "Seagull", "Sheep"])
```

The pageIndex property (Line 1) keeps track of which page the Page View Controller is currently displaying, and the album property (Lines 2-4) is the Album structure that provides the Photos information to the Page Content View Controllers.

Next, add the following lines to the end of the viewDidLoad method:

```
1    self.dataSource = self
2    if let pageContentViewController =
3        self.pageContentViewController(self.pageIndex) {
4            self.setViewControllers([pageContentViewController],
5            direction: .Forward, animated: true, completion:
6            nil)
7    }
```

Setting itself as its own data source (Line 1) means that it has adopted the UIPageViewControllerDataSource protocol, and it will then be able to provide the data necessary to display the various Page Content View Controller pages. After setting the data source, you generate the initial Page Content View Controller (Lines 2-3) using the pageIndex property (which has been initialized to 0), and initialize the Page View Controller to display the new Page Content View Controller with a Forward navigation direction (Lines 4-6).

Now that you have identified the PageViewController as its own data source, you need to add the following methods required by the UIPageViewControllerDataSource protocol to the end of the PageViewController class definition:

```
1    func pageViewController(pageViewController: UIPageViewController,
         viewControllerBeforeViewController viewController: UIViewController)
         -> UIViewController? {
2        if let contentViewController = viewController as?
         PageContentViewController {
3            return self.pageContentViewController(contentViewController.
             index - 1)
4        }
5
6        return nil
7    }
8
9    func pageViewController(pageViewController: UIPageViewController,
         viewControllerAfterViewController viewController: UIViewController)
         -> UIViewController? {
10       if let contentViewController = viewController as?
         PageContentViewController {
11           return self.pageContentViewController(contentViewController.
             index + 1)
12       }
13
14       return nil
15   }
```

When the user is swiping back and forth between pages, these two methods are called to provide the Page View Controller with the page that is before or after the current page, depending on whether the user has swiped backward or forward, accordingly. If there is no page before or after the current page (depending on which direction the user swiped), then the methods simply return nil.

Add the next two methods at the end of the class definition for the two UIPageViewControllerDataSource protocol methods, which provide the data needed to display the Page Control:

```
1    func presentationCountForPageViewController(pageViewController:
         UIPageViewController) -> Int {
2        return album.photos.count
3    }
4
5    func presentationIndexForPageViewController(pageViewController:
         UIPageViewController) -> Int {
6        return self.pageIndex
7    }
```

The first returns the total number of pages for the Page View Controller, which in this case is the number of Photos contained within the Album. The second returns the current page index so that the Page Control knows which dot should be selected.

The final method you will add to the end of the class definition is the one that returns the instantiated Page Content View Controllers for a specified page index:

```
1    func pageContentViewController(index: Int) ->
     PageContentViewController? {
2        if let contentViewController = self.storyboard?.
         instantiateViewControllerWithIdentifier
         ("PageContentViewController") as? PageContentViewController
         where index >= 0 && index < album.photos.count {
3            self.pageIndex = index
4            contentViewController.index = index
5            contentViewController.photoName = self.album.photos[index].
             name
6            return contentViewController
7        }
8
9        return nil
10   }
```

If an invalid index is passed that is beyond the number of photos within the album, the method simply returns nil (Line 9). If the index is valid, then the pageIndex property is updated with the new index (Line 3) and a new Page Content View Controller is created (Line 2) and initialized (Lines 4-5) with the index and the photo name from the associated Photo in the Album before it is returned (Line 6).

That's it! If you run the app by clicking the Build and run button in Xcode, it should run in the Apple TV simulator and display a full-screen image of a number of cows grazing, as shown in Figure 4-21.

Figure 4-21. The completed Photo Gallery app

Using the Apple TV Remote in the Simulator will allow you to swipe between the five different photos from the Animals album. Tapping on the left and right sides of the remote will allow you to scroll through the images as well.

Summary

In this chapter you created a Photo Gallery app to view multiple high-resolution photo image files using a Page View Controller. This has given you a solid starting point for learning more about the different User Interface controls available in tvOS.

In the next chapter we are going to expand on the Photo Gallery app by adding the ability for the user to choose from a list of multiple albums, and then browse the photos within them. We are also going add a custom static Top Shelf image to further showcase the contents of the app from the Home screen of the Apple TV.

Exercises

1. Try changing the Transition Style of the Page View Controller from Scroll to Page Curl and see what effect that has on the app. Try slowly swiping back and forth (and even up and down) to see how the Apple TV responds. Which style do you prefer?

2. Try adding some of your own 1080p images to the project to make your own customized Photo Gallery app.

CHAPTER 5

Adding an Album Browser to the Photo Gallery App

In Chapter 4, you started the development of a Photo Gallery Apple TV app that used a Page View Controller to allow the user to browse through a single album of full-screen photos. In this chapter, we are going to expand on that project by adding the ability for the user to choose from a list of multiple albums and then browse the photos within them. We are also going add a custom static Top Shelf image to further showcase the contents of the app from the Home screen of the Apple TV.

Table View Controllers

Table View Controllers are a common user interface element used in a number of Apple's platforms, and they provide a simple way of presenting a list of data to the user in table format. We are going to use the Table View Controller to allow the user to view and choose from a number of photo albums to browse through, as shown in Figure 5-1.

Figure 5-1. A Table View Controller containing a list of photo albums

57

A Table View Controller is in charge of populating and capturing user interface events from its embedded Table View. Each row within a Table View is referred to as a Table View Cell. The Table View Cells in Figure 5-1 each contain an image (the first image of the album), a main title (the name of the album), and a subtitle (the names of the images in the album). There are a number of default Table View Cell templates available, or you can even create your own custom templates in Interface Builder. For this project, we are going to use one of the default templates, as it will suit our needs appropriately. No point in doing extra work when you don't need to!

Adding a Table View Controller to the Photo Gallery App

You are going to want the list of albums to be the first thing that the user sees when they launch the app, so let's start by:

1. Right-clicking (or Control-clicking) the Photo Gallery group in the Project navigator and selecting New File.

2. Next, select Source underneath tvOS, and then Cocoa Touch Class, as shown in Figure 5-2.

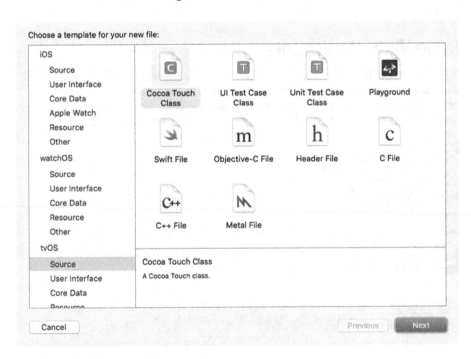

Figure 5-2. *Adding a new Cocoa Touch Class to the project*

3. Click the Next button, select UITableViewController from the Subclass drop-down list, and enter TableViewController as the Class name.

4. Make sure Swift is selected as the Language (as shown in Figure 5-3), and click Next, followed by Create to add it to the project.

Figure 5-3. *Adding the TableViewController class to the project*

Now that you have created a TableViewController class, you are going to want to:

1. Drag and drop a Table View Controller scene onto the Main.storyboard canvas to the left of the Page View Controller.

2. With the new Table View Controller scene selected, check the Is Initial View Controller check box, as shown in Figure 5-4.

59

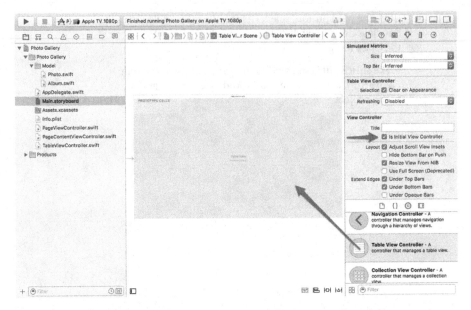

Figure 5-4. *Adding a Table View Controller scene to the Main.storyboard canvas and making it the Initial View Controller*

3. Next, with the Table View Controller scene still selected, select the Identity inspector in the Utilities area and change the Class to be the newly created TableViewController, as shown in Figure 5-5.

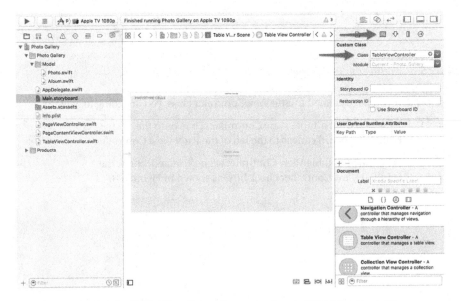

Figure 5-5. *Setting the Table View Controller scene class to TableViewController*

Now that the Table View Controller has been added to the project, you need to configure the Table View Cell to display the appropriate information for each photo album.

1. First, click the Document Outline button ▮▮ in the bottom-left corner of the canvas to show the list of scenes in the Main.storyboard, as shown in Figure 5-6.

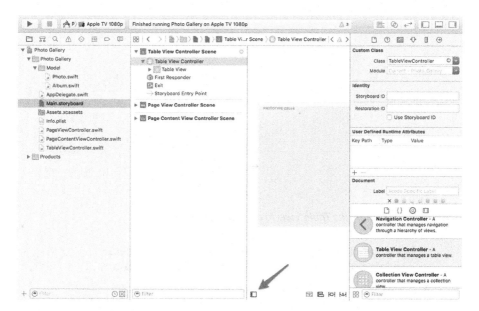

Figure 5-6. *Viewing the list of Main.storyboard scenes within the Document Outline*

2. Next, expand the Table View item underneath the Table View Controller Scene by clicking the small gray rectangle next to it, revealing the Table View Cell, as shown in Figure 5-7.

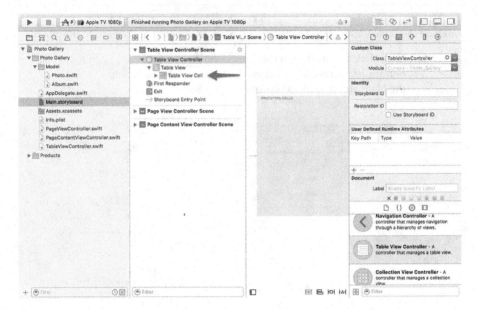

Figure 5-7. *Expanding the Table View to reveal the Table View Cell*

3. Select the Table View Cell from within the Document Outline and then select the Attributes inspector from the Utilities area.

4. Next, select Subtitle from the Style drop-down list and enter Cell as the Identifier, as shown in Figure 5-8.

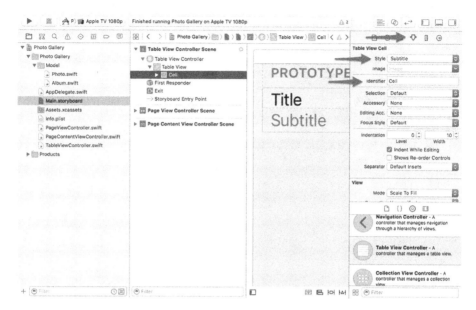

Figure 5-8. *Configuring the Table View Cell*

The Subtitle style is the default Table View Cell template that provides all of the user interface elements you need (image, main title, and subtitle) to display the list of photo albums. The Cell Identifier will be used in the TableViewController class code to identify which Table View Cell in the Table View Controller scene to use when populating the Table View. If you had more than one type of Table View Cell in the Table View, you would just need to give it a different Identifier.

The last thing you need to do in the storyboard is to add a Show segue between the Table View Cell and the Page View Controller so that when a user selects a particular photo album from the list they are able to browse through all of the photos within it.

1. To add the Show segue, first expand the Page View Controller Scene to reveal the Page View Controller.

2. Next, right-click (or Control-click) the Table View Cell and drag it to the Page View Controller, as shown in Figure 5-9.

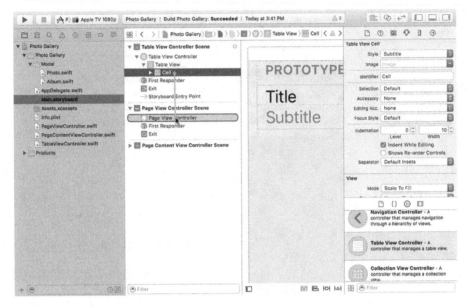

Figure 5-9. *Adding a segue between the Table View Cell and the Page View Controller*

3. Release the mouse button and choose Show under Selection Segue, as shown in Figure 5-10.

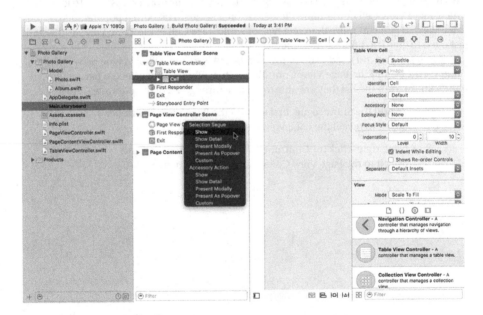

Figure 5-10. *Selecting the Show segue*

4. Select the new Show segue that was added to the Table View Controller Scene in the Document Outline and change its Identifier to SelectAlbumSegue in the Attributes inspector, as shown in Figure 5-11.

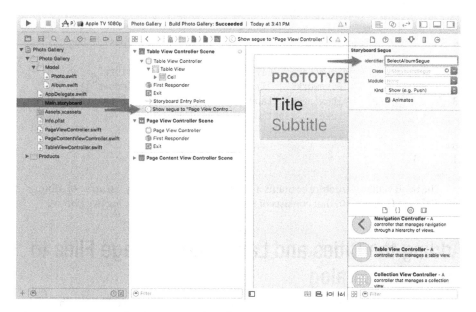

Figure 5-11. *Setting the Show segue identifier*

That completes all of the changes you need to make to the Main.storyboard, so now we can turn our attention to writing some code!

Adding the Gallery Data Model Structure

In Chapter 4, you created the data model structures to represent both a single Photo, as well as a collection of Photos within an Album. Next, you are going to define a Gallery structure to represent a collection of Albums. That way you will be able to browse through the Gallery, choose an Album, and then browse through the Album's photos.

1. To start, right-click (or Control-click) the Model group in the Project navigator and choose New File.

2. Select Source under tvOS and then select Swift File.

3. Click Next, name the file Gallery.swift, and then click Create.

Add the following code into the newly created Gallery.swift file:

```
1    import Foundation
2
3    struct Gallery {
4        var albums: [Album] {
5            return [
6                Album(name: "Animals", photoNames: ["Cows", "Dog",
                     "Horses", "Seagull", "Sheep"]),
7                Album(name: "Cities", photoNames: ["Bridge",
                     "Fireworks", "Traffic", "Village", "Windows"]),
8                Album(name: "Landscapes", photoNames: ["Coast", "Field",
                     "Lake", "Lighthouse", "Road"])
9            ]
10        }
11    }
```

The Swift Gallery structure contains a single computed property, an array of Albums called albums (Lines 4-10) that consists of three albums, each containing five photos.

Adding the Cities and Landscapes Image Files to the Asset Catalog

Now that you have defined the Gallery structure that consists of three different Albums, each containing five different Photos, you need to add those photo image files to the asset catalog, as you did in Chapter 4.

1. After downloading and unzipping the associated project files for this chapter, drag and drop the Cities and Landscapes folders containing the image files into the asset catalog to add them to the project.

2. Next, select each newly added image and change it from a Universal image to an Apple TV image, as you did in Chapter 4. Once completed, your asset catalog should look similar to that shown in Figure 5-12.

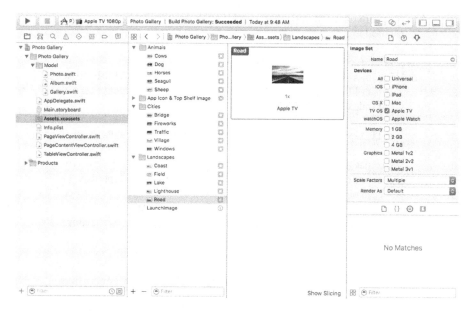

Figure 5-12. *The asset catalog containing the Animals, Cities, and Landscapes photo albums*

Completing the Photo Gallery App

Now that you have defined the Gallery structure and added the additional photo image files to the project, the last step you need to take is to finish implementing the Table View Controller that displays the list of photo albums for the user to choose from.

1. Click the TableViewController.swift file in the Project navigator and add the following line at the top of the TableViewController class declaration:

```
1       let gallery = Gallery()
```

Adding the `gallery` property to the Table View Controller will provide it with the data needed to display the list of photo albums to the user.

2. Next, scroll down to the `numberOfSectionsInTableView` data source method in the TableViewController.swift file and change the `return` 0 to `return` 1, as there is only going to be one section in this table view that will contain the three rows of photo albums.

3. Then, in the `numberOfRowsInSection` method, change the return value to the number of albums within the gallery, as shown below:

```
1       return self.gallery.albums.count
```

   4. Next, uncomment and edit the cellForRowAtIndexPath
       method to match the following:

```
1    override func tableView(tableView: UITableView,
     cellForRowAtIndexPath indexPath: NSIndexPath) -> UITableViewCell {
2        let cell = tableView.dequeueReusableCellWithIdentifier("Cell",
     forIndexPath: indexPath)
3
4        cell.textLabel?.text = self.gallery.albums[indexPath.row].name
5
6        var names = ""
7        for photo in self.gallery.albums[indexPath.row].photos {
8            names += photo.name + ", "
9        }
10       names = String(names.characters.dropLast(2))     // remove the
     last two characters of the string
11       cell.detailTextLabel?.text = names
12
13       cell.imageView?.image = UIImage(named: self.gallery.albums
     [indexPath.row].photos[0].name)
14
15       return cell
16   }
```

The cellForRowAtIndexPath method is a Table View Data Source method that is called for each Table View Cell that is displayed by a Table View. The indexPath parameter specifies which section and row within the Table View the cell is being requested for.

   In this method, you first create a new Table View Cell (Line 2) using the Cell identifier that you specified in Interface Builder earlier in the chapter. Next, you set the textLabel main title to be the name of the album for the requested row (Line 4). Then, you create a comma-delimited names String from the names of each of the photos by looping through each photo within the album (Lines 6-9) and set that to the detailTextLabel subtitle (Line 11).

■ **Note**   If you are wondering why you would remove the last two characters of the names String (Line 10) before using it, it is because you are creating it by concatenating the name of each photo, followed by a comma and a space. Since you do not want to have a comma and a space after the final name, you simply remove those last two characters after exiting the loop.

After setting the main title and subtitle strings of the cell, the final thing you need to initialize before returning it is the image, which you do by loading the image associated with the first photo in the album that is being requested (Line 13).

If you build and run the application now, you should see something similar to Figure 5-13.

Animals
Cows, Dog, Horses, Seagull, Sheep

Cities
Bridge, Fireworks, Traffic, Village, Windows

Landscapes
Coast, Field, Lake, Lighthouse, Road

Figure 5-13. *The Table View Controller showing the list of photo albums*

That looks okay, but there is a lot of empty white space underneath the list of three photo albums. You can fix this issue by making each row taller by adding the following method to the TableViewController.swift file after the cellForRowAtIndexPath method:

```
1    override func tableView(tableView: UITableView,
     heightForRowAtIndexPath indexPath: NSIndexPath) -> CGFloat {
2        return 300
3    }
```

Now when you build and run the application, you should see something similar to Figure 5-14.

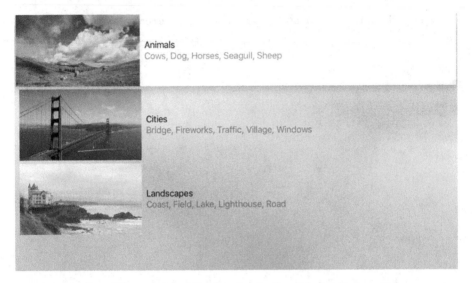

Figure 5-14. The Table View Controller showing the list of photo albums with a more acceptable amount of empty white space

If you select the Animals album using the Apple TV remote, everything works! The Animals album is displayed, and you can swipe back and forth between the photos within the album. Pressing the Menu button takes you back to the list of photo albums where you can swipe down and select either the Cities or Landscapes album and view their photos as well.

But wait! Selecting either the Cities or Landscapes album still takes us to the Animals album. Do you know why that is? What have we missed?

The reason that the Page View Controller will only show the Animals album is because it is still being initialized with that album when it is first created, and you have not yet implemented the code that passes the album selected from the Table View Controller on to the Page View Controller.

To do that, you need to uncomment and edit the prepareForSegue method located at the end of the TableViewController class declaration to contain the following:

```
1    override func prepareForSegue(segue: UIStoryboardSegue, sender:
     AnyObject?) {
2        if segue.identifier == "SelectAlbumSegue" {
3            if let pageViewController = segue.destinationViewController
             as? PageViewController, row = self.tableView.
             indexPathForSelectedRow?.row {
4                pageViewController.album = self.gallery.albums[row]
5            }
6        }
7    }
```

Remember when you connected the Table View Cell to the Page View Controller with a Show segue with the SelectAlbumSegue identifier? When a user selects a Table View Cell, the Show segue is initiated, and the prepareForSegue method is called. In the method, you first check to see if the segue's identifier is SelectedAlbumSegue (Line 2). If it is, you create local references to the Page View Controller and the row that was selected (Line 3) and initialize the album property of the Page View Controller with the album from the gallery that is indexed by the selected row (Line 4). That way, when the Page View Controller is loaded, the album property has already been initialized with the correct album data.

Great job! You have now completed the Photo Gallery app, giving users the ability to browse through a list of photo albums to view their associated full-screen photos on their widescreen HDTV.

One More Thing: Adding a Custom Static Top Shelf Image

The Photo Gallery app is now complete, but there is still something more you could do to improve it.

The Top Shelf is an area on the Apple TV Home screen that allows an app that is placed in the top row to showcase more information about itself when selected.

For example, when you select the Settings app, the Top Shelf shows a nice large image of the Settings gears icon, further indicating to the user which app is selected, as shown in Figure 5-15.

Figure 5-15. *The Settings Top Shelf image*

Selecting the Photo Gallery app next to it shows the default Apple TV Top Shelf image, as shown in Figure 5-16.

Figure 5-16. *The default Top Shelf image*

That is not very representative of the Photo Gallery app you have created. Thankfully, Apple has given developers the ability to add their own customized static Top Shelf images to their apps, giving them that additional recognition when placed in the top row of the Home screen.

Adding a custom static Top Shelf image is really quite easy.

1. Simply click the Assets.xcassets asset catalog in the Project navigator and expand the App Icon & Top Shelf Image folder.

2. Then, select Top Shelf Image and drag and drop the TopShelf.jpg image from the chapter's downloadable content to the blank 1x Apple TV space, as shown in Figure 5-17.

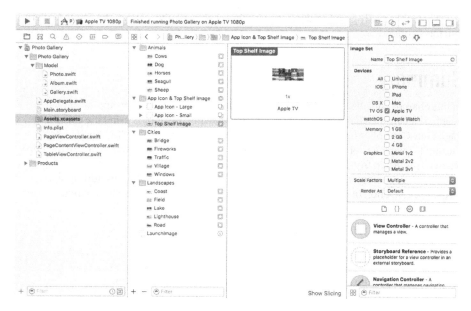

Figure 5-17. *Adding a custom static Top Shelf image*

Now, simply build and run the app, and then press the Menu button on the Apple TV remote to return to the Home screen. The Top Shelf image should now be displayed whenever the Photo Gallery app is selected while it is located in the top row of the Home screen, as shown in Figure 5-18.

Figure 5-18. *The Photo Gallery app with its custom static Top Shelf image*

That looks really great! And it is much more representative of what the Photo Gallery app has to offer.

Summary

In this chapter you added a Table View Controller to the Photo Gallery app to allow the user to select from a list of photo albums before viewing the photos using the existing Page View Controller from Chapter 4. You also added a custom static Top Shelf image to the app to give the user a better indication as to the contents and functionality of the app when it is selected from the top row of the Home screen.

In the next chapter, you will customize the Top Shelf even further by adding a scrollable collection of dynamic thumbnail images for users to choose from when launching the app.

Exercises

1. Try adding some additional albums and photos to the app from an existing album or add new albums to the gallery.

2. Try adding an additional navigation layer to the app, perhaps starting with a Table View Controller containing a list of different galleries. The galleries could contain albums organized by category, allowing the user to first choose a gallery before choosing an album to browse its photos.

CHAPTER 6

■ ■ ■

Adding a Dynamic Top Shelf to the Photo Gallery App

The Top Shelf area of the Apple TV Home screen is a great place to provide more information about an app, as well as to showcase what an app has to offer to its users. At the end Chapter 5, you added a custom static Top Shelf image to the Photo Gallery app. In this chapter, you are going to customize the Top Shelf even further by adding a scrollable collection of dynamic thumbnail images for users to choose from, as shown in Figure 6-1.

Figure 6-1. *The dynamic Top Shelf of the Photo Gallery app*

Users will be able to scroll through the collection of thumbnail images to see a preview of all of the albums within the app. Selecting any of the thumbnail images will open the Photo Gallery app, taking the user to the selected full-screen photo.

Application Extensions

You will add support for a dynamic Top Shelf by adding a new TV Services application extension that implements the TVTopShelfProvider protocol to the Photo Gallery app. App extensions are not apps themselves, but instead allow apps to provide additional functionality to the rest of the system. Apple Watch apps, custom keyboards, and Today widgets are some of the other examples of app extensions, specifically for iOS.

1. To get started, launch Xcode and open the Photo Gallery project from Chapter 5.

2. Next, select File ➤ New ➤ Target from the Xcode application menu.

3. Select Application Extension under tvOS and choose TV Services Extension, as shown in Figure 6-2.

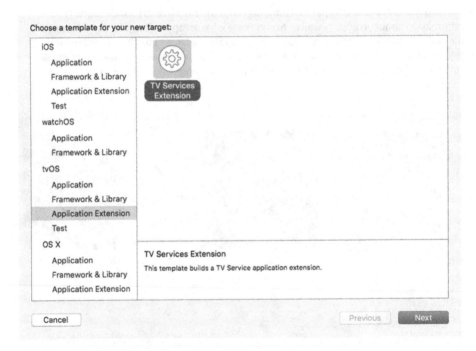

Figure 6-2. Adding a TV Services Extension to the Photo Gallery app

4. Click Next and enter Photo Gallery Extension for the Product Name, as shown in Figure 6-3.

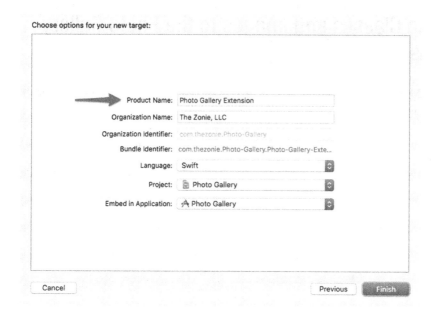

Figure 6-3. *Adding the Photo Gallery Extension to the Photo Gallery app*

5. Click Finish and then Activate, if prompted. The Photo Gallery project should now include the Photo Gallery Extension target, as shown in Figure 6-4.

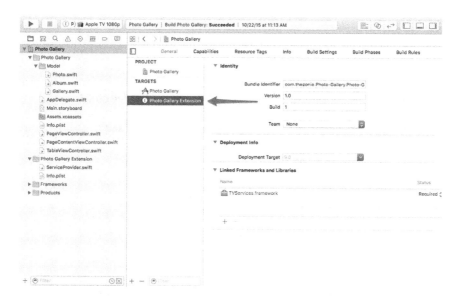

Figure 6-4. *The Photo Gallery Extension has been added to the Photo Gallery project*

Adding Classes and Images to the Photo Gallery Extension

Since the app extension is a separate target from the main Photo Gallery app, you first need to add the classes and images that it needs to know about to generate the dynamic Top Shelf data.

1. With the Photo Gallery project selected in the Project navigator, select the Photo Gallery Extension target and click the Build Phases tab, as shown in Figure 6-5.

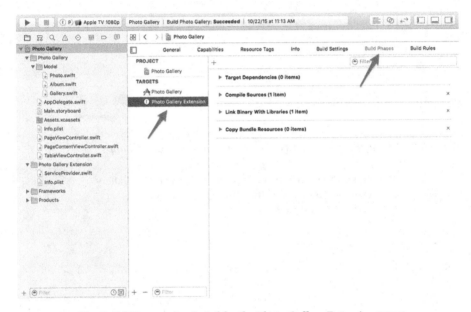

Figure 6-5. *The Build Phases tab selected for the Photo Gallery Extension target*

2. Click the triangle next to the Compile Sources item to expand it, as shown in Figure 6-6.

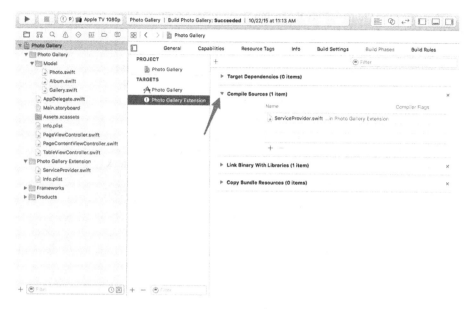

Figure 6-6. *The Compile Sources Build Phase of the Photo Gallery Extension target*

3. Click the + button at the bottom of the Compile Sources list and add the Gallery.swift, Album.swift, and Photo.swift files, as shown in Figure 6-7.

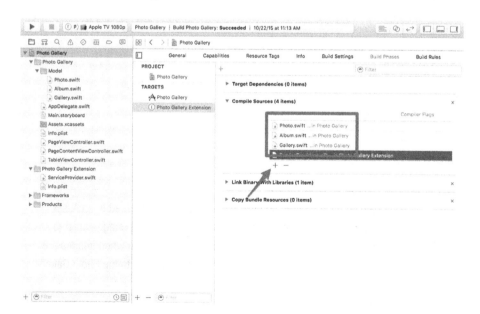

Figure 6-7. *Adding the Gallery, Album, and Photo classes to the Photo Gallery Extension*

Now that the Photo Gallery Extension knows what a Gallery, Album, and Photo are, you just need to add the actual image files to the target so that they can be used to generate the thumbnail images.

1. To add the image files to the Photo Gallery Extension, first right-click (or Control-click) the Photo Gallery Extension group, select New Group, and name it Photos.

2. Download and unzip the associated project files for this chapter, and drag and drop the Animals, Cities, and Landscapes folders onto the new Photos group in Xcode. When prompted, make sure the Copy items if needed check box is checked, the Create groups radio button is selected, and the Photo Gallery Extension target check box is checked before clicking the Finish button, as shown in Figure 6-8.

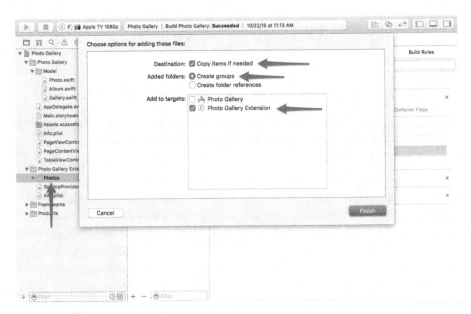

Figure 6-8. *Adding the image files to the Photo Gallery Extension target*

■ **Note**   In case you were wondering why the image files were not added to an Asset Catalog in this instance, it is because the dynamic Top Shelf thumbnail images need to be initialized using an image file URL. Image file URLs are not available when images are packaged up in an asset catalog, so that is why you instead add them to the Photo Gallery Extension target as general bundle resources.

Implementing the TVTopShelfProvider Protocol

Now that the Photo Gallery Extension target contains the necessary classes and images needed for the dynamic Top Shelf data, it is time to generate and return that data by implementing the TVTopShelfProvider protocol in the ServiceProvider.swift file.

Select the ServiceProvider.swift file from the Project navigator and replace the default topShelfItems computed property definition with the code below:

```
1    var topShelfItems: [TVContentItem] {
2        let gallery = Gallery()
3
4        var albums: [TVContentItem] = []
5
6        // create a TVContentItem for each album in the gallery
7        for albumIndex in 0..<gallery.albums.count {
8            let album = gallery.albums[albumIndex]
9
10           var photos: [TVContentItem] = []
11
12           // create a TVContentItem for each photo in the album
13           for photoIndex in 0..<album.photos.count {
14               let photo = album.photos[photoIndex]
15
16               guard let photoIdentifier =
                 TVContentIdentifier(identifier: photo.name,
                 container: nil) else { return [] }
17               guard let photoItem = TVContentItem(contentIdentifier:
                 photoIdentifier) else { return [] }
18
19               photoItem.title = photo.name
20               photoItem.imageURL = NSBundle.mainBundle().
                 URLForResource(photo.name, withExtension: ".jpg")
21               photoItem.displayURL = NSURL(string: "photogallery:vi
                 ewTopShelfItem?album=\(albumIndex)&photo=\(photoIndex)")
22
23               photos.append(photoItem)
24           }
25
26           guard let albumIdentifier = TVContentIdentifier(identifier:
                 album.name, container: nil) else { return [] }
27           guard let albumItem = TVContentItem(contentIdentifier:
                 albumIdentifier) else { return [] }
28
29           albumItem.title = album.name
30           albumItem.topShelfItems = photos
31
```

```
32              albums.append(albumItem)
33          }
34
35      return albums
36  }
```

The topShelfItems computed property is now going to return an array of TVContentItems, one for each album. Each album TVContentItem within the returned array is going to contain another array of TVContentItems, one for each photo within that album.

At the beginning of the topShelfItems computed property code block, you first create an instance of the Gallery class (Line 2) so that you can reference all of the album and photo data and information. Next, you loop over all of the albums in the gallery (Line 7) to add the associated TVContentItems to the albums array. Then, within the photos for loop, you will loop over all of the photos within that album (Line 13) to add the associated TVContentItems to the photos array.

Within the photo for loop, you first create a TVContentIdentifier using the name of the current photo (Lines 14-16), and then create the actual TVContentItem using that TVContentIdentifier (Line 17). You then set the title of the photo item to be the name of the photo (Line 19), so that it will be displayed underneath the thumbnail image when displayed in the Top Shelf, as shown in Figure 6-9.

Figure 6-9. *The title of the first TVContentItem in the Animals album is Cows*

After setting the title, you then set the imageURL (Line 20) to be the location of the associated image file that you copied to the Photo Gallery Extension earlier in the chapter. Finally, you set the displayURL (Line 21) to a specially formatted string that will be passed to the Photo Gallery application to identify which image thumbnail was selected from the Top Shelf. The displayURL string contains the photogallery scheme (which we will discuss later in the chapter) as well as the album and photo index values associated with the photo.

Once those three properties have been set for the current photo, the TVContentItem is added to the photos array at the end of the loop (Line 23).

After the photo loop is complete, the photos array contains all of the photo TVContentItems for the current album. Next, you create a TVContentIdentifier and TVContentItem for the album, just like you did for each photo (Lines 26-27). Then, you set the title of the TVContentItem to the album name (Line 29) so it will appear above each collection of image thumbnails, as shown in Figure 6-9.

After setting the topShelfItems property to be the photos array (Line 30), you add the completed album TVContentItem to the albums array at the end of the album loop (Line 32). Once you have added all of the albums to the albums array, the array is returned (Line 35).

Phew! That was quite a lot of code, but you got through it! Now, if you attempt to build and run the app extension, you will be presented with the dialog window shown in Figure 6-10. Because app extensions are not apps that can be run independently, you need to select Top Shelf from the list to see your changes reflected in the Top Shelf of your Apple TV.

Figure 6-10. *Selecting which app to run with the Photo Gallery Extension*

After clicking Run, you will see the static Top Shelf image you added in Chapter 5 replaced with the dynamic thumbnails for all of the albums and photos contained within the gallery. Swiping up on the Apple TV remote when the Photo Gallery app is selected allows you to focus on the Top Shelf items and swipe back and forth between all of the available photos.

Launching the Photo Gallery App from a Top Shelf Thumbnail Image

Browsing through all of the thumbnails is great, but what we really want to do is click on one of those thumbnails to view the selected image within the Photo Gallery app. To allow the Photo Gallery Extension to do this, you are first going to have to make some changes to the main Photo Gallery app.

1. In the Project navigator, select the Info.plist file that is within the Photo Gallery group, not the one within the Photo Gallery Extension group, as shown in Figure 6-11.

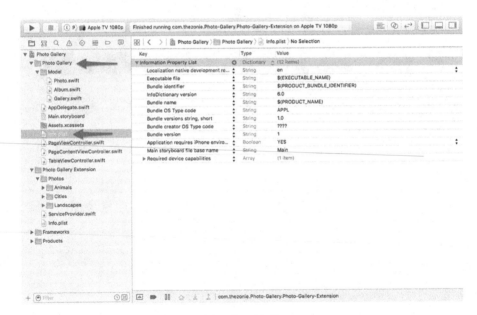

Figure 6-11. *Selecting the Info.plist of the Photo Gallery app*

2. Once the Info.plist has been selected, hover the mouse pointer over the last item in the list, click the + button that appears to add a new key to it, and choose URL types from the list, as shown in Figure 6-12.

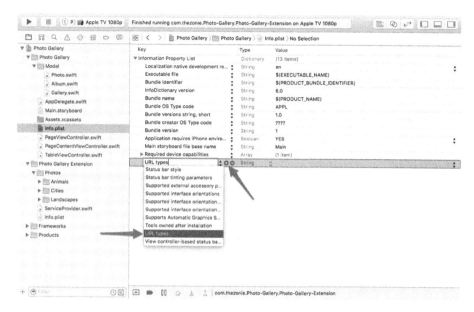

Figure 6-12. *Adding the URL types item to the Info.plist*

3. After adding the URL types key to the Info.plist, click the small gray triangle next to it to expand it, revealing the Item 0 subkey.

4. Then click the small gray triangle next to the Item 0 key to reveal the URL identifier subkey underneath it.

5. Click in the Value column of the URL identifier item and change the value to Photo Gallery URL, as shown in Figure 6-13.

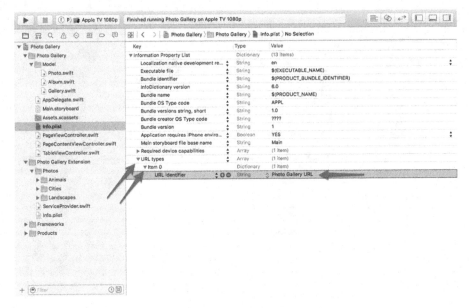

Figure 6-13. *Changing the URL identifier to Photo Gallery URL*

6. Next, click the + button from within the URL identifier item and select URL Schemes from the list, as shown in Figure 6-14.

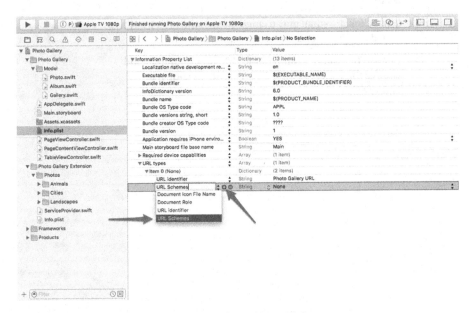

Figure 6-14. *Adding the URL Schemes subkey to the Info.plist*

7. Click the gray triangle next to the URL Schemes key to expand it to reveal its Item 0 subkey. Change the value of Item 0 to be photogallery, as shown in Figure 6-15.

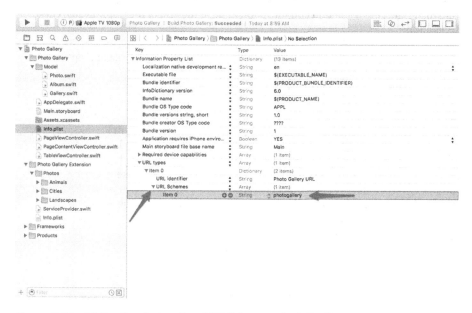

Figure 6-15. *Adding the photogallery URL Scheme to the Info.plist*

Adding the photogallery URL Scheme to the Info.plist registers that scheme (as mentioned earlier in the chapter) with the system. Now, whenever any URL that begins with photogallery is opened on the Apple TV, it will be opened by the Photo Gallery app.

Build and run the app extension and select one of the thumbnails from the Top Shelf. The Photo Gallery app is now launched, but the image that was selected is not yet being displayed. To accomplish this, you first need to tell the Photo Gallery application how to handle the URL information that is passed to the app when it is opened from a Top Shelf thumbnail image.

Handling URLs

When an Apple TV app is launched from a matching URL scheme, the URL is passed to a UIApplicationDelegate protocol method called openURL. Open the AppDelegate.swift file from the Project navigator and add the follow code to the end of the AppDelegate class declaration:

```
1    func application(app: UIApplication, openURL url: NSURL, options:
     [String : AnyObject]) -> Bool {
2        var albumIndex: Int?
3        var photoIndex: Int?
4
5        // extract the album and photo index from the url
6        guard let components = NSURLComponents(URL: url,
         resolvingAgainstBaseURL: false) else { return true }
7        guard let queryItems = components.queryItems else { return true }
8        for queryItem in queryItems {
9            if let valueString = queryItem.value, value =
             Int(valueString) {
10               if queryItem.name == "album" {
11                   albumIndex = value
12               }
13               else if queryItem.name == "photo" {
14                   photoIndex = value
15               }
16           }
17       }
18
19       // if the album and photo index values have been set, view that
         photo
20       if albumIndex != nil && photoIndex != nil {
21           // pass the album and photo index values to the
             TableViewController
22           if let tableViewController = window?.rootViewController as?
             TableViewController {
23               tableViewController.viewSelectedTopShelfPhoto(
                 photoIndex!, inAlbum: albumIndex!)
24           }
25       }
26
27       return true
28   }
```

In this method, you first use the URL passed in from the Top Shelf TVContentItem to create an NSURLComponents object (Line 6) in order to extract the albumIndex and photoIndex values from the URL string (Lines 8-17). Then, if both of those values have been set (Line 20), you find the TableViewController object from the main app window (Line 22) and pass it to its viewSelectedTopShelfPhoto method (Line 23).

Completing the Photo Gallery App

Now you need to make the appropriate changes to the TableViewController
class to handle this new method being called from the App Delegate. Open the
TableViewController.swift file and add the following line of code to the top of the class
declaration, beneath the gallery property declaration:

```
1       var selectedTopShelfItem: (albumIndex: Int?, photoIndex: Int?) =
        (nil, nil)
```

This defines a tuple property containing two integers, one for the album index and
one for the photo index. Initially both of the index values are nil, indicating that a Top
Shelf item has not been selected.

Next, define the viewSelectedTopShelfPhoto method by adding the following code
to the end of the class declaration:

```
1       func viewSelectedTopShelfPhoto(photo: Int, inAlbum album: Int) {
2           // save the selected top shelf album photo index values
3           self.selectedTopShelfItem = (album, photo)
4
5           // if I am not the presented view controller, pop back
6           if let presentedViewController = self.presentedViewController {
7               presentedViewController.dismissViewControllerAnimated(false,
                completion: nil)
8           }
9           else {
10              self.checkSelectedTopShelfItem()
11          }
12      }
```

In this method, you first store the album and photo index values within the new
selectedTopShelfItem tuple property (Line 3). Then, you check to see what the current
state of the app's view controller hierarchy is. If a user has previously left the app viewing
another full-screen image (Line 6), then you would want to dismiss the presented
PageViewController object (Line 7) before viewing the newly selected photo. If there is no
presentedViewController set (Line 9), then that means there is no PageViewController
object to dismiss, so the user can continue to view the selected photo (Line 10).

Next, add the following code to the end of the class declaration to check whether a
Top Shelf item has been selected, and if so, performing the appropriate action:

```
1       func checkSelectedTopShelfItem() {
2           if let albumIndex = self.selectedTopShelfItem.albumIndex {
3               self.tableView.selectRowAtIndexPath(NSIndexPath(forRow:
                albumIndex, inSection: 0), animated: false,
                scrollPosition: .None)
4               self.performSegueWithIdentifier("SelectAlbumSegue", sender: nil)
5           }
6       }
```

In this method, if the album index within the `selectedTopShelfItem` is set (Line 2), you can then select that row in the table view (Line 3) and manually perform the `SelectAlbumSegue` that is used when a user clicks one of the albums from the list to browse the photos within it (Line 4).

When a user selects a Top Shelf image and the app is opened, depending on its previous state, a PageViewController object may need to be dismissed. If that is the case, the app needs to be notified when that process is complete so that it can continue to view the selected Top Shelf item photo. The easiest way to do this is to override the Table View Controller's `viewDidAppear` method by adding the following code to the TableViewController.swift file after the `viewDidLoad` method declaration:

```
1    override func viewDidAppear(animated: Bool) {
2        super.viewDidAppear(animated)
3        self.checkSelectedTopShelfItem()
4    }
```

Now, whenever the Table View Controller appears, the `selectedTopShelfItem` is checked (Line 3).

The final change you have to make is to pass the selected photo index to the PageViewController object from within the `prepareForSegue` method of the Table View Controller. Add the following changes to the TableViewController.swift file so that the `prepareForSegue` looks like this:

```
1    override func prepareForSegue(segue: UIStoryboardSegue, sender:
     AnyObject?) {
2        if segue.identifier == "SelectAlbumSegue" {
3            if let pageViewController = segue.destinationViewController
             as? PageViewController, row = self.tableView.
             indexPathForSelectedRow?.row {
4                pageViewController.album = self.gallery.albums[row]
5
6                // if there is a selected photo index set it as well and
                 then reset it
7                if let photoIndex = self.selectedTopShelfItem.photoIndex {
8                    pageViewController.pageIndex = photoIndex
9                    self.selectedTopShelfItem = (nil, nil)
10               }
11           }
12       }
13   }
```

Now, if the segue matches the `SelectAlbumSegue` identifier (Line 2), after a Page View Controller is created (Line 3) and its album has been initialized (Line 4), its pageIndex is set to the photoIndex of the `selectedTopShelfItem` (Lines 7-8) so that the appropriate image will be selected once the app is launched. Finally, the `selectedTopShelfItem` is reset back to its uninitialized state (Line 9).

Now, when you select a thumbnail image from the Top Shelf, the Photo Gallery app is launched and the appropriate album is displayed with the appropriate photo already selected.

Summary

Congratulations! Over the course of the past few chapters, you have created a Photo Gallery app that enables users to select and view photos from within a number of different photo albums, in addition to viewing those photos when selecting them from the Top Shelf area of the Apple TV Home screen.

You have learned about using Page View Controllers, Table View Controllers, and Application Extensions on tvOS, all using Swift. The knowledge you have gained throughout these chapters will provide you with a great foundation for developing other apps in the future using these aspects of tvOS development.

In the next chapter, we will explore how to store app information on the Apple TV itself, as well as how to store and sync data to the cloud.

Exercises

1. By default, the imageShape property of a TVContentItem is Square for the default Sectioned TVTopShelfContentStyle. The other options available are Poster and HDTV. Make the appropriate changes to the Photo Gallery Extension to utilize these different styles to see which style you like best.

2. You can mix and match the TVTopShelfContentStyle values throughout the TVContentItems displayed in the Top Shelf. You currently have three albums, and there are three styles available. Make the appropriate changes to the Photo Gallery Extension to use a different TVTopShelfContentStyle for each album, or perhaps choose a random style for each and every photo to really give your app a unique look!

■ ■ ■

CHAPTER 7

Storing and Sharing Data

The Apple TV has undergone quite an evolution when it comes to storage. The original Apple TV came with a standard 40GB or 160GB hard drive. The Apple TV would use that storage for holding movies, TV shows, and music locally on the Apple TV. For the next two generations of the Apple TV, Apple removed the hard drive completely. Instead, the Apple TV was equipped with 8GB of flash storage. These boxes lacked the ability to locally store any media; instead movies, TV shows, and music all had to be streamed either from a local computer or across the Internet. With the fourth-generation, Apple has released a hybrid solution. The new Apple TVs come in either 32GB or 64GB versions, but apps are still required to stream most of their data and content. Apple currently limits an app to a total of 200MB of local storage, but this data are temporary and can be removed when the app is quit.

This chapter will discuss methods for storing information locally on the Apple TV, as well as how to sync data using iCloud.

Preferences

There are some things to consider when deciding where to store certain kinds of information. The easiest way to store information is within the preferences file, but this method has some downsides.

All of the data are both read and written at the same time. If you are going to be writing often or writing large amounts of data, this could take time and slow down your application. As a general rule, your preferences file should never be larger than 100KB. Currently, the preference file is capped at 500KB for tvOS, but a developer should consider other storage methods long before reaching that limit.

The preferences file is really nothing more than a standardized file with accompanying classes and methods to store application-specific information. A preference would be, for example, the sorting column and direction (ascending/descending) of a list. Anything that is generally customizable within an app should be stored in its preferences file.

Writing Preferences

Apple has provided developers with the NSUserDefaults class; this class makes it easy to read and write preferences for the iPhone, AppleTV, and Mac OS X. The great thing is that, in this case, you can use the same code for iOS and Mac OS X. The only difference between the two implementations is the location of the preferences file.

All you need to do to write preferences is to create an NSUserDefaults object. This is done with the following code:

```
let prefs: NSUserDefaults = NSUserDefaults.standardUserDefaults()
```

This instantiates the prefs object so you can use it to set preference values. Next, you need to set the preference keys for the values that you want to save. The BookStore app example will be used to demonstrate specific instructions throughout this chapter. When running a bookstore, you might want to save a username or password in the preferences. You also might want to save things such as a default book category or recent searches. The preferences file is a great place to store this type of information because this is the kind of information that needs to be read only when the application is launched.

Also, on tvOS, it is often necessary to save your current state. If a person is using your application presses the home button, you want to be able to bring them back to the exact place they were in your application when they are done with their phone call.

Once you have instantiated the object, you can just call setObjectforKey to save your preferences. If you wanted to save the username of sherlock.holmes, you would call the following line of code:

```
prefs.setObject("sherlock.holmes", forKey: "username")
```

You can use setInteger, setDouble, setBool, setFloat, and setURL instead of setObject, depending on the type of information you are storing in the preferences file. Let's say you store the number of books a user wants to see in the list. Here is an example of using setInteger to store this preference:

```
prefs.setInteger(10, forKey:"booksInList")
```

After a certain period of time, your app will automatically write changes to the preferences file.

With just three lines of code, you are able to create a preference object, set two preference values, and write the preferences file. It is an easy and clean process. Here is all of the code:

```
let prefs: NSUserDefaults = NSUserDefaults.standardUserDefaults()
prefs.setObject("sherlock.holmes", forKey: "username")
prefs.setInteger(10, forKey:"booksInList")
```

Reading Preferences

Reading preferences is similar to writing preferences. Just like with writing, the first step is to obtain the NSUserDefaults object. This is done in the same way as it was done in the writing process:

```
let prefs: NSUserDefaults = NSUserDefaults.standardUserDefaults()
```

Now that you have the object, you are able to access the preference values that are set. For writing, you use the setObject syntax; for reading, you use the stringForKey method. You can use the stringForKey method because the value you put in the preference was a String. In the writing example, you set preferences for the username and for the number of books in the list to display. You can read those preferences by using the following simple lines of code:

```
var username = prefs.stringForKey("username")
var booksInList = prefs.integerForKey("booksInList")
```

Pay close attention to what is happening in each of these lines. You start by declaring the variable username, which is a string. This variable will be used to store the preference value of the username you stored in the preferences. Then, you just assign it to the value of the preference username.

iCloud

The iCloud is a service provided by Apple that allows developers to sync data and information across multiple devices. This is especially helpful with tvOS apps since the local storage is limited. In order to implement iCloud storage in an app, a developer must first make sure that their app has iCloud enabled. To do this, visit the Apple Developer Portal (http://developer.apple.com). Sign in and click Member Center in the top right corner of the screen. Then click Certificates, Identifiers & Profiles, as shown in Figure 7-1.

Figure 7-1. *Selecting Certifications, Identifiers & Profiles*

Next, select Identifiers under the iOS section. Then select App IDs from the left-hand side, as shown in Figure 7-2.

Figure 7-2. *Select App IDs*

Find the App ID in the list and select it. This will bring up a list of the Application Services available in the app, as shown in Figure 7-3.

Figure 7-3. *Current App ID entitlement*

Click the Edit button at the bottom of the list to add iCloud support. The check boxes seen in Figure 7-4 allow a developer to enable iCloud. Check the box and the app should now have access to iCloud.

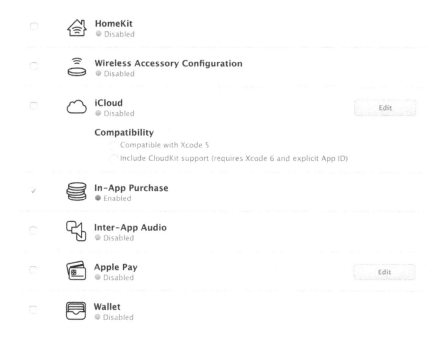

Figure 7-4. *Enabling iCloud*

It is also possible to add iCloud capabilities through Xcode. On the left-hand side, select your project, then select the active target, and choose the Capabilities tab. You will then see a screen similar to that shown in Figure 7-5.

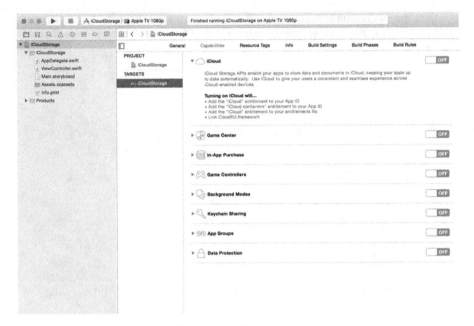

Figure 7-5. *Adding iCloud capabilities through Xcode*

You can turn iCloud on and off through this method also. Now with iCloud enabled, it is possible to easily store your data in the cloud.

iCloud KVS

There are two ways to store information in iCloud. One way is to implement iCloud KVS or key-value storage. The second way is by using CloudKit. CloudKit is more powerful and more complicated. It will be discussed in Chapter 8. iCloud KVS is very similar to NSUserDefaults and should only be used for storing very small amounts of data. Apple caps the iCloud KVS storage at 1MB. The major benefit to using iCloud KVS is that the data are automatically synced across all iCloud devices within the same account.

The iCloud KVS is implemented very similarly to NSUserDefaults. It has the same limitations and issues, but is also used in a very similar way. The code to implement iCloud KVS is fairly simple. Start by creating a new Xcode project. Make sure tvOS Application is selected. For this project, use Single View Application, as shown in Figure 7-6.

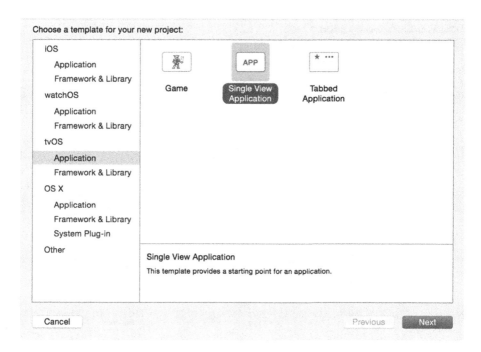

Figure 7-6. *Creating a new project*

Click Next and enter the name and details of the app. We used the name iCloudStorage, as shown in Figure 7-7.

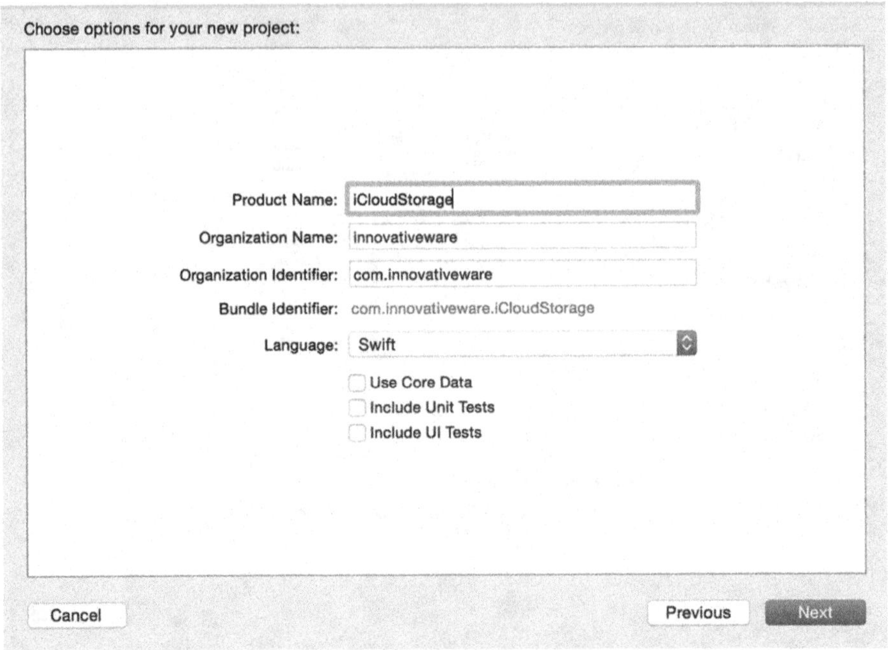

Choose options for your new project:

Product Name:	iCloudStorage
Organization Name:	innovativeware
Organization Identifier:	com.innovativeware
Bundle Identifier:	com.innovativeware.iCloudStorage
Language:	Swift

☐ Use Core Data
☐ Include Unit Tests
☐ Include UI Tests

Cancel   Previous   Next

Figure 7-7. Naming you project

Once the project save location is selected, Xcode will open the project. Select the AppDelegate.swift file from the left-hand side of the list of files. We will be implementing the iCloud KVS in the AppDelegate.swift file.

■ **Note**   In a real-world project, it is better to create a singleton manager to handle your data syncing. Singletons are classes that are only instantiated a single time. They are easier to extend and access. A singleton is implemented in Swift through the use of static class variables.

At the top of the AppDelegate class, under the window variable, you need to add the following two variables:

```
var iCloudKeyStore: NSUbiquitousKeyValueStore = NSUbiquitousKeyValueStore.
defaultStore()
var iCloudString: String = String()
```

The first variable, iCloudKeyStore, is an NSUbiquitousKeyValueStore value. This basically means that it is like an NSUserDefaults that is stored in the cloud. The second variable, iCloudString, is a string that will be used to store the value synced through iCloud.

Next, you will modify the application:didFinishLaunchingWithOptions: method. You need to tell the iCloud service to alert you once your NSUbiquitousKeyValueStore is changed by another app. This way you can reload your iCloudString from the key store. Add the following lines:

```
NSNotificationCenter.defaultCenter().addObserver(self,
            selector: "iCloudDataChanged:",
            name:  NSUbiquitousKeyValueStoreDidChangeExternallyNotification,
            object: iCloudKeyStore)
```

This code tells the notification center to call the method "iCloudDataChanged:" on your AppDelegate object whenever your key store changes values in any way. Notice the iCloudKeyStore variable is passed in. It is possible to have multiple key stores and receive notifications for them separately. Next, you will add the code to check the key store for the string:

```
27    if let savedString = iCloudKeyStore.stringForKey("myString") {
28        iCloudString = savedString
29    } else {
30        iCloudKeyStore.setString("Testing", forKey: "myString")
31        iCloudKeyStore.synchronize()
32    }
```

Let's walk through this code. The name of the key you are using in the NSUbiquitousKeyValueStore is myString. Obviously, when creating a real app, you will want to use descriptive titles for your keys such as username or default view. Line 27 attempts to set the value of savedString to the key myString from the key store. If this succeeds, that means the key exists. You then assign the value of savedString to the iCloudString variable.

If you are unable to pull myString from the key store, this means the key has yet to be set in the cloud. You then need to tell the key store to store a value for this key. Line 30 calls the method setString on the key store and passes in a String (Testing) and a key (myString). Line 31 then tells the key store to sync the data immediately with the cloud. By default, an NSUbiquitousKeyValueStore will sync its data on a regular basis, but by calling the synchronize method, you can force the sync immediately.

■ **Note**   In this example, you use `setString` and `stringForKey` to set and retrieve the string value from the key store. Apple provides different methods for different data types. The following retrieval methods are available:

- arrayForKey:
- boolForKey:
- dataForKey:
- dictionaryForKey:
- doubleForKey:
- longLongForKey:
- objectForKey:
- stringForKey:

The AppDelegate.swift file should now look like the one shown in Figure 7-8.

Figure 7-8. *AppDelegate.swift file*

There is still one problem with our code. You have told the NSNotificationCenter to call the method iCloudDataChanged on your appdelegate, but this method has not yet been defined. Add the following method to the AppDelegate.swift file:

```
func iCloudDataChanged() {
    if let myString = iCloudKeyStore.stringForKey("myString") {
        iCloudString = myString
    }
}
```

This method merely assigns the value of myString from the key store to the iCloudString variable.

You can now compile and run your app.

■ **Note** You may receive a console message at run time similar to the following error:

NSUbiquitousKeyValueStore error: com.innovativeware.iCloudStorage has no valid com.apple.developer.ubiquity-kvstore-identifier entitlement

This means you have not set up your entitlements for your app correctly.

Summary

In this chapter, you learned how to handle local storage on the Apple TV. You also learned how to add iCloud storage. We showed you how to become alerted to a change in the iCloud storage and how to send and receive values to and from it.

Exercises

1. Add a number to your NSUbiquitousKeyValueStore.

2. Add an Array to your cloud storage.

CHAPTER 8

■ ■ ■

CloudKit

Chapter 7 discussed storing preferences both locally on the AppleTV and in the cloud using NSUserDefaults and NSUbiquitousKeyValueStore. This method works great for storing small pieces of information, but what happens when the app needs to store a significant amount of information? What happens when an app needs to search or sort this type of information? This is where CloudKit comes in. CloudKit is a framework provided by Apple that allows developers to easily sync databases between different devices.

CloudKit is currently available only for iOS , Mac OS X, and tvOS devices. Apple has provided CloudKit JS. CloudKit JS looks to enable web apps and any other apps that can implement javascript to hook into existing CloudKit databases. This chapter will not cover CloudKit JS since it is not needed on tvOS.

Considerations for Using CloudKit

CloudKit is virtually free! Apple currently provides developers with 10GB of asset storage and 2GB data transfer per month for free with a developer account. They also provide 100MB of database storage and 40 requests per second. All of this storage is provided for free, but that is not the best part. Apple increases all four of the limitations as you add additional users. For example, with 100,000 active users, the asset storage is increased to 25TB. As an app scales even larger, Apple will provide up to 1 petabyte (PB or 1000 terabytes or 1,000,000 gigabytes) of asset storage and 400 requests per second. Most apps will be able to implement CloudKit without paying any monthly fees. Apple provides pricing and limits details on their iCloud for Developers site (https://developer.apple.com/icloud/).

CloudKit data are either stored as public or private. Public data are available to all of those with the app. Private data are available only to specific iCloud accounts. As a developer designs their app, they need to consider what types of data are available to all and which data are account specific.

CloudKit Containers

All CloudKit data are separated into different containers. Containers will hold all of the databases and information for each CloudKit-enabled app. Each app will have its own container. It is, however, possible to share containers with different apps from the same developer. The container ID will match the app's bundle ID. Apple provides a class called CKContainer for accessing the different containers.

The default app container can be accessed by using the following code:

```
var myContainer = CKContainer.defaultContainer()
```

Creating a custom container is easy.

1. Head to the Apple developer home page (http://developer. apple.com) and log in. Select Member Center ➤ Certificates, Identifiers, & Profiles. Then select Identifiers under iOS Apps. This will bring up a menu on the left-hand side similar to that shown in Figure 8-1. Select iCloud Containers.

Figure 8-1. *Select iCloud Containers*

2.   Click the Add button, as shown in Figure 8-2.

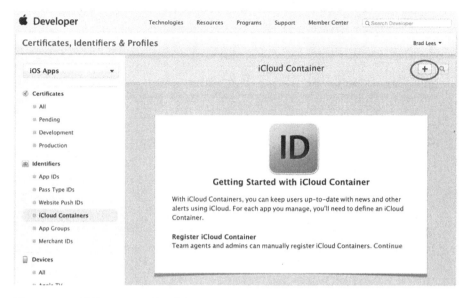

Figure 8-2. *Adding a new iCloud Container*

3.   You will then be prompted to enter a description and an identifier, as shown in Figure 8-3. The description is only used to display what is stored in the container. The identifier is necessary for accessing the container.

Figure 8-3. Creating a new Container

4. Enter CloudKit Demo2 for the description and enter a unique string for the identifier. Identifiers tend to follow the pattern of iCloud.com.companyID.containerName. The identifier will be used to access the container in the different apps. Click Continue and you will see a screen similar to that shown in Figure 8-4.

Figure 8-4. *Finished Creating the CloudKit Container*

Click the Register button and the container is now ready to be used. To access this container, use the following code:

```
myContainer = CKContainer.init("iCloud.com.inno.cloudkit2")
```

Databases

The container ID will need to be replaced with whatever you used to register your container in the previous step. Each container will contain a public and a private database. The public database will contain information and assets that are shared among all of the instances of the database. All users will have read and write access to the public database through your app.

■ **Note** A developer needs to be careful when dealing with the public database. If one user is able to delete items from it, all other users will be affected.

The private database is only accessible to the current user. The user will have to enter their username and password, but then they will have read and write access to that database.

CloudKit Databases

Apple has provided the CKDatabase class for accessing the databases. Once a container has been connected, it is easy to access the public and private databases. Use the following code to access the private database:

```
var myContainer = CKContainer.defaultContainer()
  var publicDatabase: CKDatabase = myContainer.publicCloudDatabase
var privateDatabase: CKDatabase = myContainer.privateCloudDatabase
```

Database Records

A CKRecord is used to store data in your database. Each CKRecord has different pieces of data stored as key-value pairs. Records should be separated into distinct tables or record types for each type of data. For example, for a bookstore, it would make sense to have a record type of Book and a separate record type of Author. Each record type will have a name and fields associated with it. Table 8-1 from Apple's documentation (https://developer.apple.com/library/tvos/documentation/ DataManagement/Conceptual/CloudKitQuickStart/CreatingaSchemabySavingRecords/ CreatingaSchemabySavingRecords.html) shows the possible field types for a record.

Table 8-1. *Possible Field Types for a Record*

Field Type	Class	Description
Asset	CKAsset	A large file that is associated with a record but stored separately
Bytes	NSData	A wrapper for byte buffers that is stored with the record
Date/Time	NSDate	A single point in time
Double	NSNumber	A double
Int(64)	NSNumber	An integer
Location	CLLocation	A geographical coordinate and altitude
Reference	CKReference	A relationship from one object to another
String	NSString	An immutable text string
List	NSArray	Arrays of any of the above field types

Creating a record is a fairly easy process. The following code would accomplish this:

```
let newBook = CKRecord(recordType: "Book")
```

This creates a new constant called newBook that is of the type Book. Now, you are able to set values of fields on this newBook constant:

```
newBook.setValue("The Hobbit", forKey: "title")
newBook.setValue("J. R. R. Tolkien", forKey: "author")
```

This code sets the title of the book equal to "The Hobbit". The author of the book was also set. Now that the CKRecord of the book is all set, it can be saved to the database. You would save this record to the public database in this case with the following code:

```
27 CKContainer.defaultContainer().publicCloudDatabase ().saveRecord(newBook,
   completionHandler: { (record: CKRecord?, error: NSError?) in
28
29          if error != nil {
30              print("There was an error")
31
32          } else {
33              print("Record Saved Successfully")
34          }
35    })
```

Line 27 tells the public database of the default container to save this record. It also passes in a *completion handler*, which is a method that will run when the first method is complete. The completion method, in this case, merely tells you if there was an issue saving the record.

Example CloudKit App

Let's create a CloudKit tvOS app. Launch Xcode and select Create a new Xcode project. You will be prompted with the type of project. Select tvOS on the left-hand side and select Single View Application, as shown in Figure 8-5. Click Next.

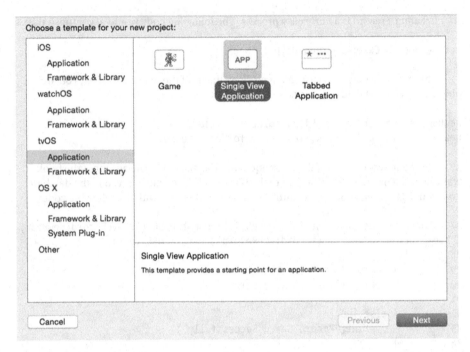

Figure 8-5. *Create a Single View tvOS application*

On the next screen, fill in the name of your application. We are using CKBookStore for the name. The Organization Name and Organization Identifier should already be filled in. Make sure the language selected is Swift. None of the check boxes need to be checked (see Figure 8-6). Then click Next.

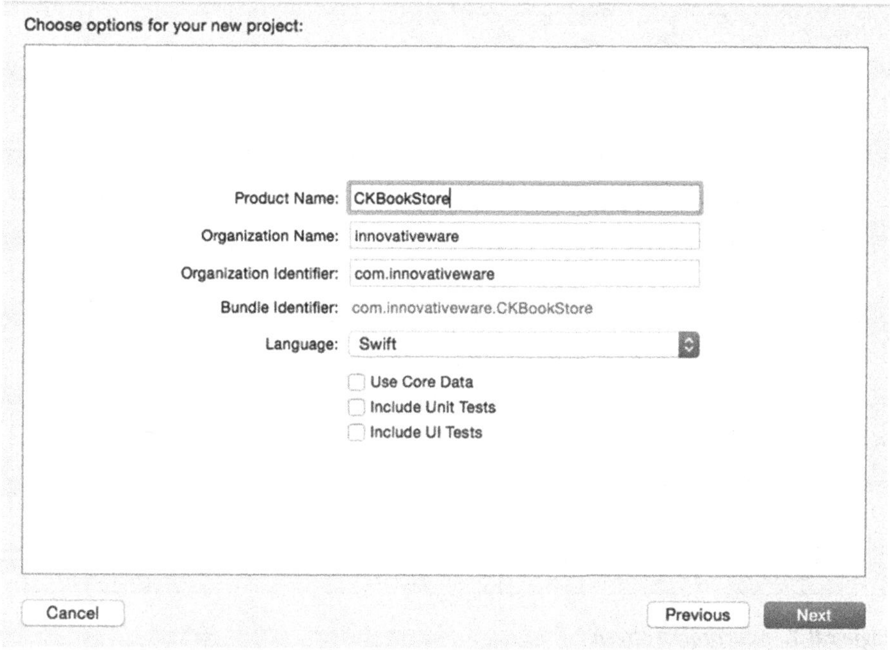

Figure 8-6. *Naming the project*

You will be prompted to save your project. Select a location you can easily access. Once Xcode opens the project, you will see something similar to Figure 8-7.

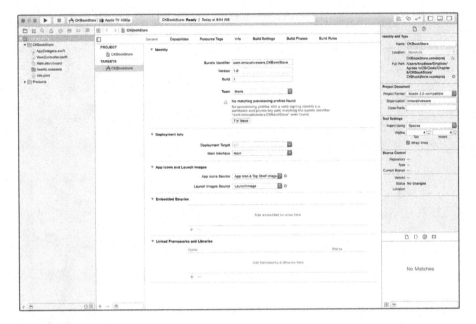

Figure 8-7. *New project screen*

By default, the project is selected in the Project Navigator on the left, and the active target will be selected in the targets list. This allows you to change settings and enable CloudKit as the active target. Select Capabilities from the Targets menu, as shown in Figure 8-8.

Figure 8-8. *Select Capabilities in the Targets menu*

Expand the arrow next to iCloud. Toggle the switch to On. If your user account belongs to multiple teams, Xcode will prompt you to select the team to connect with this application. Make sure CloudKit is checked under the Services heading. Your screen should now look like Figure 8-9. The Container IDs

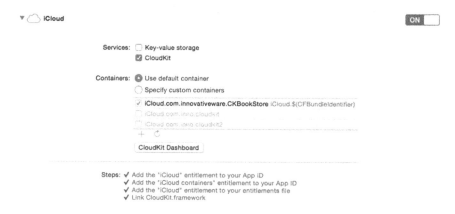

Figure 8-9. *Successfully added CloudKit to the app*

For this app, the default container will be used. If additional containers are available for this app, they will be displayed and are able to be selected on this screen. Apple also provides a link to the CloudKit Dashboard. This is a web interface Apple provides developers for administering CloudKit databases. Click the CloudKit Dashboard.

■ **Note** The CloudKit Dashboard works best in Safari.

After entering your developer credentials, you should see a screen similar to Figure 8-10.

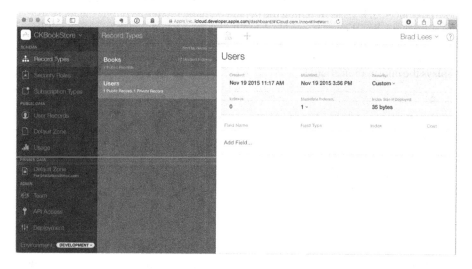

Figure 8-10. *CloudKit Dashboard*

You won't be doing anything in the Dashboard for now, but it is useful for managing record types, queries, and records. You will be using it later in the chapter.

For now, let's go back to the app and click the AppDelegate.swift file in the Project Navigator. You need to add a method to create book records in CloudKit. Under the import UIKit line, add the following line:

```
import CloudKit
```

Now add the following method at the end of the file, but inside the closing brace:

```
45 func setupBooks() {
46
47         let newBook = CKRecord(recordType: "Books")
48         newBook["title"] = "The Hobbit"
49         newBook["author"] = "J. R. R. Tolkien"
50
51         CKContainer.defaultContainer().publicCloudDatabase.
           saveRecord(newBook) { (record: CKRecord?, error: NSError?) ->
           Void in
52             print("Done")
53             if(error != nil) {
54                 print("error")
55                 print(error.debugDescription)
56             }
57         }
58     }
```

Line 45 creates the method called setupBooks. Line 47 creates a new CKRecord of the type Book. Lines 48 and 49 add a title and an author to this book. Line 51 is a little more complicated. It starts by telling the default container to tell its public database to save this record. You then pass in a block method to be executed when the save is either completed or fails. You are passing two parameters. The first one is the record you tried to save and the second one is the error, if any. Line 53 checks to see if there was an error and displays the information about it.

■ **Note**   If the save function fails, many times it is because the user is not logged into their iCloud account on the device.

To call this method, add the following line to the application didFinishLaunchingWithOptions at the beginning of the file:

```
setupBooks()
```

This will add a book to your cloud every time the app is launched. This is a good way to test things out, but you will definitely want to change this in the real world. Once done, your AppDelegate.swift file should look like the one shown in Figure 8-11.

```swift
//
//  AppDelegate.swift
//  CKBookStore
//
//  Created by Brad Lees on 11/19/15.
//  Copyright © 2015 innovativeware. All rights reserved.
//

import UIKit
import CloudKit

@UIApplicationMain
class AppDelegate: UIResponder, UIApplicationDelegate {

    var window: UIWindow?


    func application(application: UIApplication, didFinishLaunchingWithOptions launchOptions:
        [NSObject: AnyObject]?) -> Bool {
        // Override point for customization after application launch.
        setupBooks()|
        return true
    }

    func applicationWillResignActive(application: UIApplication) {
        // Sent when the application is about to move from active to inactive state. This can occur
            for certain types of temporary interruptions (such as an incoming phone call or SMS
            message) or when the user quits the application and it begins the transition to the
            background state.
        // Use this method to pause ongoing tasks, disable timers, and throttle down OpenGL ES frame
            rates. Games should use this method to pause the game.
    }

    func applicationDidEnterBackground(application: UIApplication) {
        // Use this method to release shared resources, save user data, invalidate timers, and store
            enough application state information to restore your application to its current state in
            case it is terminated later.
        // If your application supports background execution, this method is called instead of
            applicationWillTerminate: when the user quits.
    }

    func applicationWillEnterForeground(application: UIApplication) {
        // Called as part of the transition from the background to the inactive state; here you can
            undo many of the changes made on entering the background.
    }

    func applicationDidBecomeActive(application: UIApplication) {
        // Restart any tasks that were paused (or not yet started) while the application was inactive.
            If the application was previously in the background, optionally refresh the user
            interface.
    }

    func applicationWillTerminate(application: UIApplication) {
        // Called when the application is about to terminate. Save data if appropriate. See also
            applicationDidEnterBackground:.
    }

    func setupBooks() {

        let newBook = CKRecord(recordType: "Books")
        newBook.setValue("The Hobbit", forKey: "title")
        newBook.setValue("J. R. R. Tolkien", forKey: "author")

        CKContainer.defaultContainer().publicCloudDatabase.saveRecord(newBook) { (record, error) ->
            Void in
            print("Done")
            if(error != nil) {
                print("error")
                print(error.debugDescription)
            }
        }
    }

}
```

Figure 8-11. *Finished AppDelegate*

Run your app and see if the record was successfully saved. It should be. Open the Console log in Xcode to verify the word "Done." If you do see an error in the log, it is likely the user will need to log into iCloud on the device.

Now that you have saved this book, you need to work on getting all of the book records from the cloud. You will retrieve the cloud information in the ViewController. swift. Click ViewController.swift. Add the import CloudKit line at the top of the file like we did in the AppDelegate.swift file. In the viewDidLoad method, add the following code to the bottom of the method:

```
20        let myPredicate: NSPredicate = NSPredicate(value: true)
21        let myQuery: CKQuery = CKQuery(recordType: "Books", predicate:
          myPredicate)
22
23        CKContainer.defaultContainer().publicCloudDatabase.
          performQuery(myQuery, inZoneWithID: nil) {
24            results, error in
25            if error != nil {
26                print("Error")
27                print(error.debugDescription)
28            } else {
29                print(results)
30            }
31        }
```

Line 20 creates an NSPredicate, which is used to create a search query. NSPredicates are also used with Core Data. They are a powerful way to query. The NSPredicate only queries the records where value=true, and this is how you query all of the records. True is always true, so this will create an NSPredicate to return all of the records.

Line 21 creates a CKQuery by passing in the record type and the NSPredicate you created in the previous line. A CKQuery can also have an NSSortDescriptor. This allows you to sort the data you are retrieving back from CloudKit.

Line 23 tells the public database to perform the query. It is possible to segregate your records into different zones. That is beyond the scope of this book, so here just send in nil to the zone identifier parameter.

Lines 24 to 33 are the block methods to be executed once the query is complete. You can now check to see if there is an error. If something failed, it will then display the error in the log. If there is no error, you can print the records you received into the log. Once complete, your code should look like that shown in Figure 8-12.

```
import UIKit
import CloudKit

class ViewController: UIViewController {

    override func viewDidLoad() {
        super.viewDidLoad()
        // Do any additional setup after loading the view, typically from a nib.

        let myPredicate: NSPredicate = NSPredicate(value: true)
        let myQuery: CKQuery = CKQuery(recordType: "Books", predicate: myPredicate)

        CKContainer.defaultContainer().publicCloudDatabase.performQuery(myQuery, inZoneWithID: nil) {
            results, error in
            if error != nil {
                print("Error")
                print(error.debugDescription)
            } else {
                print(results)
            }
        }
    }

}
```

Figure 8-12. *Finished viewDidLoad*

If you now run this app as it stands, you will receive an error. You now need to go to the CloudKit Dashboard located at `https://icloud.developer.apple.com/dashboard/`.

One the left-hand side, click Record Types, then Books, as shown in Figure 8-13. The number of public records will change depending on the number of times you have run the app.

Figure 8-13. *Selecting Books Record Type*

You will now see a screen similar to that shown in Figure 8-14.

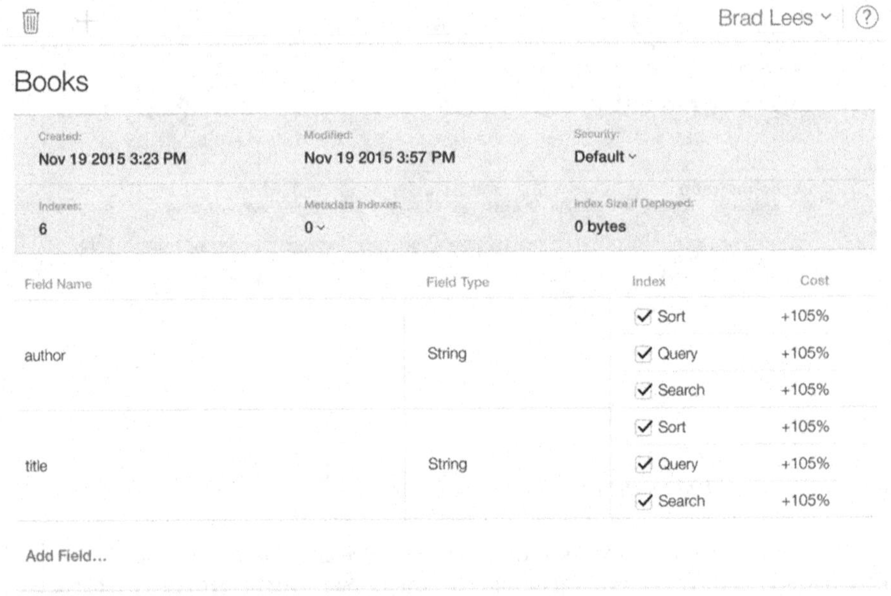

🗑 +   Brad Lees ⌄ ⑦

Books

Created:	Modified:	Security:
Nov 19 2015 3:23 PM	Nov 19 2015 3:57 PM	Default ⌄

Indexes:	Metadata Indexes:	Index Size if Deployed:
6	0 ⌄	0 bytes

Field Name	Field Type	Index	Cost
		✓ Sort	+105%
author	String	✓ Query	+105%
		✓ Search	+105%
		✓ Sort	+105%
title	String	✓ Query	+105%
		✓ Search	+105%

Add Field...

Figure 8-14. *Books details*

Click the downward arrow underneath Metadata Indexes and check the box next to Record ID, as shown in Figure 8-15. This allows your application to access these metadata as part of a query. You will notice, Apple will inform you of the cost of selecting that index. It will add 5% to your storage requirements. This is fine in this case, but when designing for large CloudKit applications, size will need to be considered.

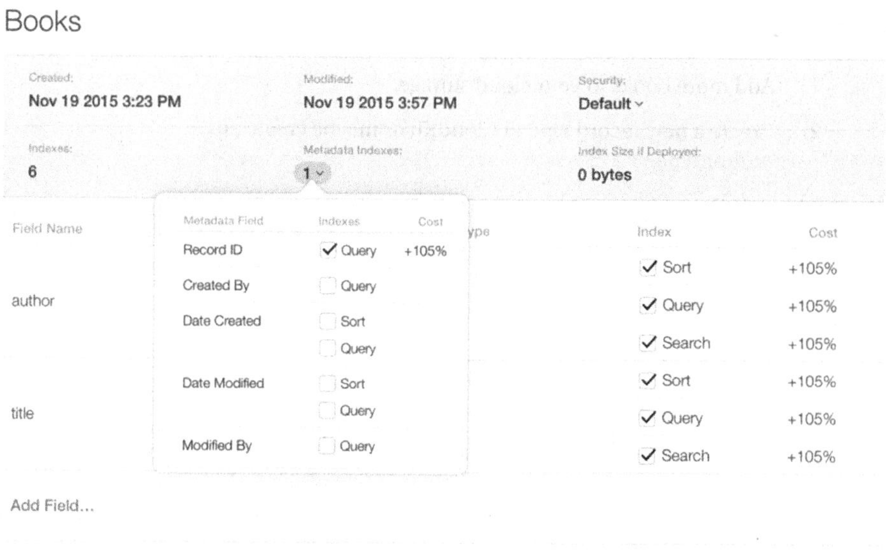

Books

	Created: Nov 19 2015 3:23 PM		Modified: Nov 19 2015 3:57 PM		Security: Default ⌄

| | Indexes:
6 | | Metadata Indexes:
1 ⌄ | | Index Size if Deployed:
0 bytes |

Field Name						Index	Cost

	Metadata Field	**Indexes**	**Cost**	
	Record ID	✓ Query	+105%	
	Created By	☐ Query		
author	Date Created	☐ Sort		
		☐ Query		
	Date Modified	☐ Sort		
title		☐ Query		
	Modified By	☐ Query		

Index	Cost
✓ Sort	+105%
✓ Query	+105%
✓ Search	+105%
✓ Sort	+105%
✓ Query	+105%
✓ Search	+105%

Add Field…

Figure 8-15. *Creating a Record ID index*

Now click the Save button at the bottom right corner of the screen. Launch your app and you should receive a log similar to that shown in Figure 8-16. There will be one line for each time you called setupBooks().

```
Optional([<CKRecord: 0x7fab71d292e0; recordType=Books, recordID=03E1AB2C-8ABC-4825-8E5B-933C4340443B:(_defaultZone:__defaultOwner__), recordChangeTag=ih6tybr0, values={
    author = "J. R. R. Tolkien";
    title = "The Hobbit";
}>, <CKRecord: 0x7fab71e04900; recordType=Books, recordID=6B1A1CA6-B868-4482-85A3-0F0253CA7176:(_defaultZone:__defaultOwner__), recordChangeTag=ih6u768n, values={
    author = "J. R. R. Tolkien";
    title = "The Hobbit";
}>, <CKRecord: 0x7fab71e04a10; recordType=Books, recordID=88360FCB-938E-45D5-97F4-EA8ED969C9B0:(_defaultZone:__defaultOwner__), recordChangeTag=ih6tyvyd, values={
    author = "J. R. R. Tolkien";
    title = "The Hobbit";
}>, <CKRecord: 0x7fab71e04e00; recordType=Books, recordID=8C2BE4F1-696B-4E3E-9780-2C467D0E2E6C:(_defaultZone:__defaultOwner__), recordChangeTag=ih6u7sbl, values={
    author = "J. R. R. Tolkien";
    title = "The Hobbit";
}>, <CKRecord: 0x7fab71e04d00; recordType=Books, recordID=9BB79CCA-FC90-4DD1-B4A7-274E47F61057:(_defaultZone:__defaultOwner__), recordChangeTag=ih6u8h3u, values={
    author = "J. R. R. Tolkien";
    title = "The Hobbit";
}>, <CKRecord: 0x7fab71e050b0; recordType=Books, recordID=C5C0CA23-81D2-4D4A-A121-67809CE0D6B1:(_defaultZone:__defaultOwner__), recordChangeTag=ih6t0ukp, values={
    author = "J. R. R. Tolkien";
    title = "The Hobbit";
}>, <CKRecord: 0x7fab71e05700; recordType=Books, recordID=EB0346E6-84DC-4428-9146-5384C6A12C37:(_defaultZone:__defaultOwner__), recordChangeTag=ih720f0u, values={
    author = "J. R. R. Tolkien";
    title = "The Hobbit";
}>])
```

Figure 8-16. *Retrieving records from CloudKit*

Summary

In this chapter you learned about CloudKit and the basic objects required to access CloudKit. You learned about the CloudKit Developer Console and how to view records and record types in a web browser. You also created an app to save CloudKit records and retrieve them.

This book as shown you how to begin development for the new AppleTV. We have shown some of the familiar iOS controls and classes and also highlighted some of the ones that are different for tvOS. Due to the tvOS lack of local storage, we also spent time demonstrating how to store and retrieve data from iCloud.

Exercises

1. Add more books to your cloud storage.

2. Create a new record type in CloudKit or maybe create an Author type.

Index

Get the eBook for only $5!

Why limit yourself?

Now you can take the weightless companion with you wherever you go and access your content on your PC, phone, tablet, or reader.

Since you've purchased this print book, we're happy to offer you the eBook in all 3 formats for just $5.

Convenient and fully searchable, the PDF version enables you to easily find and copy code—or perform examples by quickly toggling between instructions and applications. The MOBI format is ideal for your Kindle, while the ePUB can be utilized on a variety of mobile devices.

To learn more, go to www.apress.com/companion or contact support@apress.com.

Printed in the United States
By Bookmasters